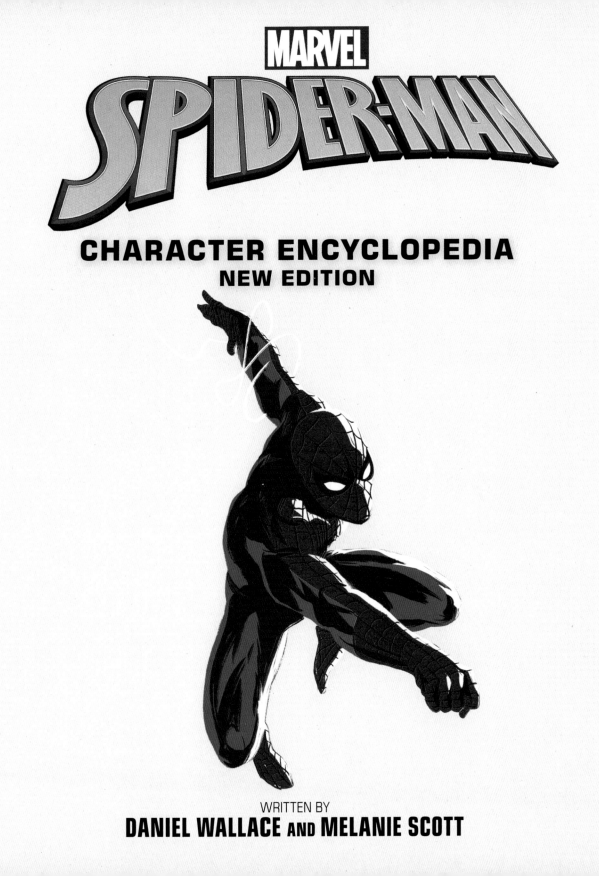

MARVEL
SPIDER-MAN

CHARACTER ENCYCLOPEDIA
NEW EDITION

WRITTEN BY
DANIEL WALLACE AND **MELANIE SCOTT**

INTRODUCTION

The wall-crawling, web-swinging Spider-Man is one of the greatest heroes of them all. Peter Parker—now fighting beside his young ally Miles Morales—has secretly protected New York City and the world from a host of Super Villains, such as Doctor Octopus, the Green Goblin, Venom, and the Sinister Six. Meet Spidey's closest friends, including the Avengers and the Fantastic Four, and come face-to-face with his worst enemies in this one-of-a-kind visual guide.

CONTENTS

This book contains more than 200 characters with links to Spider-Man. Each page is filled with revealing facts. Apart from Peter Parker and Miles Morales—featured in the opening pages—characters appear in alphabetical order according to their first names or aliases. Some characters, such as Norman Osborn, whose significance goes far beyond the Green Goblin, have two entries. Use the contents list below to swing straight to the Super Hero or Villain of your choice.

PETER PARKER

Having the secret identity of Spider-Man has caused Peter Parker plenty of headaches, but he knows that his powers mean that he can protect his loved ones and the citizens of New York City. Peter has worked as a photographer and science correspondent for *The Daily Bugle*, has been a researcher at Horizon Labs, and has even owned his own multinational corporation, Parker Industries.

Peter never expected the bite of a radioactive spider to react with his DNA the way it did, but he has made the most of his gifts.

Peter often curses what he calls the "Parker Luck," a phenomenon in which whenever something goes right in his life, something else will go wrong. Often the Parker Luck is a side effect of Peter trying to juggle his double life.

As a photographer, Peter dresses in clothing that won't draw attention.

BRAINS AND HARD WORK
Peter has always struggled for money. For years he supported his Aunt May with his earnings from *The Daily Bugle*, and he has also used his engineering talents to earn money on the side. Peter doesn't accept payment for his work as Spider-Man.

Although his identity is theoretically secret, a lot of Spider-Man's close associates know that he is Peter Parker.

SPIDER-MAN

Spidey swings high above New York City, his home and base of operations for Super Hero adventures.

Spider-Man was just an ordinary teenager when he gained super-powers from a radioactive spider. Learning the hard way that with great power comes great responsibility, he was motivated by the death of his Uncle Ben to use his abilities to do the right thing and protect those who could not protect themselves. The wall-crawling, web-slinging hero fights courageously to keep his city free of crime.

Spidey's web-shooters are mechanical devices.

Spider-Man has perfect control over his wall-crawling grip.

HERO OR MENACE?
Spider-Man is a misunderstood figure in the city he calls home, thanks to the past negative press coverage from J. Jonah Jameson and *The Daily Bugle*. Yet he never gives up, and is good friends with well-respected teams such as the Avengers and the Fantastic Four.

VITAL STATS
REAL NAME: Peter Benjamin Parker
OCCUPATION: Super Hero, photographer, inventor
BASE: New York City
HEIGHT: 5 ft 10 in (1.78 m)
WEIGHT: 135 lbs (61 kg)
EYES: Hazel **HAIR:** Brown
ORIGIN: Human mutate; granted the proportionate abilities of a spider by a radioactive spider bite
POWERS: Spider-Man can cling to most surfaces and has superhuman strength, speed, and reflexes. His "spider-sense" warns him of danger, and his wrist web-shooters spray strong web-lines.

ENERGY PROJECTION	STRENGTH	DURABILITY	FIGHTING SKILL	INTELLIGENCE	SPEED	POWER RANK
1	4	3	4	4	3	

MILES MORALES

Miles Morales is a student at the Brooklyn Visions Academy for gifted children. Great things are expected of him by his teachers and family, but Miles has to juggle the demands of his schoolwork with the more life-threatening demands of being a hero—Spider-Man. Miles grows up in the New York City of Earth-1610, but after the multiverse is destroyed and remade, he and his close friends and family are transplanted to Earth-616.

The arrival of Miles' little sister Billie is a blessing for the Morales family, but his connection to her makes her a potential target for Super Villains.

Miles is from Brooklyn in New York City. Although he has been known to fight bad guys across the five boroughs of the city and beyond, he is first and foremost a protector of his own neighborhood.

Miles has a network of family and close friends to support him.

DEAR DIARY
Confiding his innermost thoughts to his journal is a way for Miles to manage the mental burden of his dual life. At first it is just an assignment from his creative writing teacher, but Miles soon realizes the benefits of having somewhere secret and unhackable where he can write out his problems.

Miles has a creative streak—in his spare time he likes to draw and write.

As well as his spider-powers, Spider-Man can emit bioelectrical blasts and also has a "cloaking" power that is similar to invisibility.

SPIDER-MAN

Spider-powered Miles Morales took up the mantle of Spider-Man when the Peter Parker of his reality was killed in action. He continued his heroic career when his own universe was destroyed, becoming a protector of the Earth-616 version of Brooklyn. Spider-Man also fights planetary and even multiversal threats as part of teams like the Avengers, the Champions, and the Order of the Web.

VITAL STATS
REAL NAME: Miles Gonzalo Morales
OCCUPATION: Student, vigilante
BASE: Brooklyn, New York City
HEIGHT: 5 ft 2 in (1.57 m)
WEIGHT: 125 lbs (56.7 kg)
EYES: Brown
HAIR: Black
ORIGIN: Human mutate; gained powers after being bitten by a genetically enhanced spider
POWERS: Miles has the proportionate strength of a spider and other spider-powers such as wall-crawling; he can fire bioelectric blasts from his hands, and he has a camouflage ability.

His new costume is made from super-strong Van Dyne fabric.

SURVIVOR
Miles is originally from Earth-1610, the Ultimate Universe, but after this reality is destroyed he escapes to Battleworld. After showing kindness to the Molecule Man, Miles is given a new home by him, on Earth-616. Here he can learn from the example of Peter Parker, who had died in Miles' home universe.

Spider-Man's look, styled in red and black, has become iconic.

ENERGY PROJECTION	STRENGTH	DURABILITY	FIGHTING SKILL	INTELLIGENCE	SPEED
2	4	3	3	2	3

POWER RANK

SPIDER-MAN COSTUMES

As well as their main Spider-Man suits, both Peter Parker and Miles Morales have worn a variety of costumes during their heroic careers. Some were specially designed upgrades, like the Iron Spider armor built by Tony Stark, some came about purely by accident, like Miles' first Spidey costume, while others had altogether more extraterrestrial origins!

2

1

PETER PARKER'S COSTUMES

1. **Spider Armor:** Bulletproof suit made from flexible metal.

2. **Black Suit:** Revealed to be an alien symbiote in disguise.

3. **Iron Spider Armor:** Advanced suit with targeting systems and four arms.

4. **Stealth Suit:** Bends light and sound around its wearer.

3

4

MILES MORALES' COSTUMES

1. **First Costume:**
Second-hand Spider-Man
Hallowe'en costume given to
Miles by his friend Ganke Lee.

2. **Ultimate Suit:** Given to
Miles by S.H.I.E.L.D. as
official approval of his role
as the new Spider-Man.

3. **Captain Universe:**
When Miles gained the
Uni-Power during the second
war against the Inheritors his
look was cosmically changed.

4. **Shadow Spider:**
Miles ended up in Weirdworld
with the Champions and was
changed into the stealthy
Shadow Spider.

THE SPIDER-VERSE

At the center of the multiverse sits the Master Weaver, spinning and protecting the Web of Life and Destiny. Its threads span out and connect every reality that has ever existed, and only certain special beings have the power to traverse its strands and change the fates of their worlds—the spider-totems. Together, they and the universes they inhabit represent the Spider-Verse.

It is a revelation to Spider-Man and his allies on Earth-616 that there are countless other worlds protected by spider-powered heroes.

KEY UNIVERSES

Earth-616: The Prime Universe, home to an unusually large amount of spider-totems.

Earth-001: Loomworld, where the Web of Life and Destiny is located; also the Inheritors' longtime base.

Earth-13: Believed to be a safe zone for spider-powered beings, protected by a Spider-Man with the powers of Captain Universe.

Earth-65: Ghost-Spider (Gwen Stacy) lives in this reality, in which Peter Parker has died.

Earth-982: Mayday Parker takes over from her fallen father Peter to become Spider-Woman and protect her baby brother Benjy.

Earth-1610: Original home of Miles Morales, this reality is destroyed during the Incursions and not restored.

Earth-8311: A reality populated by cartoon-like talking animals, protected by Spider-Ham (Peter Porker).

Earth-90214: A Depression-hit and crime-riddled reality where Spider-Man Noir is one of the few Super Heroes.

THE CHOSEN

The Spider-Verse has many secrets. It transpires that there are special spider-beings with a particular connection to the Web of Life and Destiny, known as the Other, the Scion, and the Bride. It later emerges that there is also a Pattern-Maker, with the power to remake the Web if it breaks.

For every reality in the multiverse, there seems to be a spider-powered being. Some resemble each other while others are wildly different. Some are named Peter Parker, but in other worlds it is his friends and family who have trodden the path of the hero. Whoever they are, there are often fundamental events or philosophies linking the spider-heroes—family tragedy, for example, or the philosophy that with great power comes great responsibility.

WEB-WARRIORS

The Spider-Army is an alliance of many different spider-heroes from across the multiverse, who came together to fight the existential threat of the Inheritors. After victory the team disbands, but a core group of heroes remain to be the watchmen for the Spider-Verse and the Web of Life and Destiny—they are the Web-Warriors.

The infinite variety of the multiverse is reflected in the seemingly limitless number of its weird and wonderful spider-powered heroes.

KEY MEMBERS

Billy Braddock of Earth-833: Spider-UK is the leader of the Captain Britain Corps and later the Web-Warriors. After his reality is destroyed he remains on Earth-001 to watch over those realities that have lost their spider heroes.

Anya Corazon of Earth-616: Anya is given her powers by the mysterious Spider Society. She volunteers to stay in Earth-001 to protect the Spider-Verse.

Mayday Parker of Earth-982: Daughter of Peter Parker and Mary Jane Watson, Mayday inherits her powers from her father.

Gwen Stacy of Earth-65: From a world in which Peter Parker died, Gwen got powers from a spider bite and fights crime as Ghost-Spider.

Peter Parker of Earth-90214: Forged in a world still suffered under the Great Depression, "Spider-Man Noir" is an investigative reporter and a ruthless vigilante.

Peter Porker of Earth-8311: Peter Porker was a spider who was bitten by a radioactive pig, and uses his powers to protect the cartoon-like reality of Earth-8311.

DAVIS

Aaron Davis fell into petty crime as a youngster, soon discovering that he had a flair for thievery. As one of the most skilled thieves around, he was in demand as a robber-for-hire and mercenary. However, he was killed on Earth-1610 after a clash with Spider-Man—Aaron's nephew, Miles Morales. When the multiverse was restored, Aaron found himself given a second chance on Earth-616.

Aaron's relationship with his brother Jeff has been rocky, but when Jeff recognizes that Aaron is trying to go straight and build bridges with his family, he is there to support him.

VITAL STATS

REAL NAME: Aaron Davis
OCCUPATION: Mercenary
BASE: Brooklyn, New York City
HEIGHT: 6 ft 1 in (1.86 m)
WEIGHT: 195 lbs (88 kg)
EYES: Brown
HAIR: Black
ORIGIN: Human, originally from parallel reality of Earth-1610
POWERS: Aaron has no super-powers, although he occasionally uses high-tech equipment to enhance his abilities. He is a master thief and a skilled martial artist.

Without a high-tech suit, Aaron is just a normal—albeit very athletic—man.

Miles Morales is always welcome at his uncle Aaron's apartment.

PAST CRIMES

As Aaron's criminal career flourished, he managed to acquire high-tech equipment to assist him in his nefarious activities. He has used both the Iron Spider and the Prowler suits, but is now trying to leave his past behind and straighten up.

POWER RANK	ENERGY PROJECTION	STRENGTH	DURABILITY	FIGHTING SKILL	INTELLIGENCE	SPEED
	1	2	1	4	2	1

ANASTASIA KRAVINOFF

Like her father, Kraven the Hunter, Ana Kravinoff has enhanced abilities thanks to a mixture of mysterious serums. Although her father had little to do with her during her childhood, Ana teaches herself to become a hunter by reading his diary and using it as a training manual. She becomes an expert tracker and extremely skilled both in hand-to-hand combat and with various weapons.

Spider-Man realizes that Ana Kravinoff is an enemy to be reckoned with when she uses pure strength to break out of his webbing.

INHUMAN BEHAVIOR
Ana is disgusted to discover that she has Inhuman ancestry on her mother's side, believing that her blood is no longer pure and not good enough for the Kravinoff name. However, she comes to believe that she should embrace her heritage and whatever new powers it might offer her.

Ana uses many weapons to deadly effect, including a variety of blades and throwing weapons such as bolas.

She is a master in Krav Maga, a martial art developed by combining the most efficient techniques of other disciplines.

VITAL STATS
REAL NAME:
Anastasia "Ana" Kravinoff
OCCUPATION: Hunter
BASE: Mobile
HEIGHT: 5 ft 4 in (1.63 m)
WEIGHT: 120 lbs (54 kg)
EYES: Blue **HAIR:** Blond
ORIGIN: The daughter of Kraven the Hunter, trained to emulate him in every way. Ana inherits from her family a hatred of Spider-Man
POWERS: Ana has super-strength and speed, enhanced senses due to consumption of magical elixirs, is an expert tracker, and is highly skilled in hand-to-hand combat.

ENERGY PROJECTION	STRENGTH	DURABILITY	FIGHTING SKILL	INTELLIGENCE	SPEED	POWER RANK
1	4	3	5	3	3	

13

ANNA MARIA MARCONI

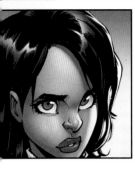

Anna Maria Marconi is a student at Empire State University when she agrees to tutor Peter Parker, although she doesn't realize that Peter's body has been taken over by Doctor Octopus. It is Otto Octavius who recognizes Anna Maria's abilities and hires her for Parker Industries, but when the real Peter Parker returns he keeps Marconi on as a vital and trusted part of his operations.

Anna Maria is a spectacular "science chef," using her knowledge of chemistry and physics to perfect her culinary creations. Cookery is also therapeutic for her.

VITAL STATS

REAL NAME: Anna Maria Marconi
OCCUPATION: Scientist
BASE: New York City
HEIGHT: 3 ft 11 in (1.19 m)
WEIGHT: 80 lbs (36 kg)
EYES: Brown
HAIR: Black
ORIGIN: Human; student at Empire State University who becomes a scientist and employee of Parker Industries
POWERS: Anna Maria possesses a genius-level intellect.

Anna Maria Marconi has a formidable intellect and is a key employee at Parker Industries.

MISTAKEN IDENTITY

Anna Maria believes herself to be in a relationship with Peter Parker, and she is devastated when she discovers that the man she loves is really a Super Villain. Villain or not, Doctor Octopus genuinely loves Anna, and sees her as one of the few people intellectually worthy of his respect.

The Jackal offers to clone a body "without defects" for Anna Maria, who angrily retorts that she is already perfect.

POWER RANK	ENERGY PROJECTION	STRENGTH	DURABILITY	FIGHTING SKILL	INTELLIGENCE	SPEED
	1	1	1	1	4	1

ANTI-VENOM

Anti-Venom's intentions may be good, but his appearance is fearsome, and people fear alien symbiotes like him.

When Eddie Brock removed the alien symbiote called Venom from his body, tiny traces of it remained. These remnants, mutated by the healing powers of Mister Negative, bonded with Eddie's white blood cells to create Anti-Venom. Despite their long history as enemies, he and Spider-Man joined forces.

Anti-Vemon's senses are sharper than any human's.

HEALING AND HELPING
Eddie Brock has worked hard to make up for the crimes he committed as Venom. Anti-Venom's healing abilities saved the day when New York's citizens suddenly gained spider-powers, and the city descended into chaos as "Spider-Island."

Anti-Venom's touch can transfer healing microbes.

VITAL STATS
REAL NAME: None
OCCUPATION: Vigilante, anti-hero
BASE: Mobile
HEIGHT: Variable **WEIGHT:** Variable
EYES: Orange **HAIR:** None
ORIGIN: Symbiote mutate; Martin Li's Lightforce powers merged the remnants of the Venom symbiote in Eddie's body with his white blood cells, creating a new symbiote: Anti-Venom
POWERS: Anti-Venom has superhuman strength, durability, and stamina, as well as incredible healing powers. He can wall-crawl and shoot out parts of himself in the form of webs or tentacles.

ENERGY PROJECTION	STRENGTH	DURABILITY	FIGHTING SKILL	INTELLIGENCE	SPEED
1	4		4	3	2

POWER RANK

AUNT MAY PARKER

Peter Parker's Aunt May has been like a mother to him since he was a boy. When her husband, Ben Parker, was killed by a burglar, Aunt May raised Peter on her own as he secretly started his life as a Super Hero. While May is a doting aunt who loves to make her famous meatloaf for family visits, she is also very tough, perhaps a result of her many brushes with costumed villains over the years.

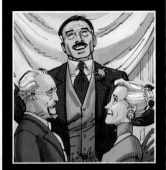

Aunt May later married Jay Jameson, father of *The Daily Bugle*'s J. Jonah Jameson. Sadly the marriage was short-lived, and May was widowed once again.

VITAL STATS

REAL NAME: Maybelle Parker-Jameson
OCCUPATION: Retired
BASE: New York City
HEIGHT: 5 ft 5 in (1.65 m)
WEIGHT: 110 lbs (49.9 kg)
EYES: Blue
HAIR: Gray
ORIGIN: Human
POWERS: Aunt May has no special combat skills or super-powers, but she is a smart, resourceful woman and an excellent judge of character.

Being close to Peter has often placed Aunt May in danger.

LIFE CHANGES
Aunt May is a practical, down-to-earth homemaker. Losing his parents, and later his Uncle Ben, taught Peter to value the role that she plays in his life, offering a glimpse of stability and normality in his otherwise chaotic world.

Learning Peter's secret didn't change Aunt May's love for him.

POWER RANK	ENERGY PROJECTION	STRENGTH	DURABILITY	FIGHTING SKILL	INTELLIGENCE	SPEED
	1	1	1	1	2	1

AVENGERS

With a cry of "Avengers Assemble," the world's greatest Super Hero team races into action! The Avengers take on Super Villains that are too powerful for a single hero to defeat. Both Peter Parker and Miles Morales have been members of Earth's Mightiest Heroes, with Parker even bankrolling the team for a while during his time as a wealthy CEO.

KEY MEMBERS

1. **Captain America:** Has an indestructible shield.

2. **Wolverine:** Has adamantium claws and healing powers.

3. **Hulk:** Possesses incredible strength and durability.

4. **Falcon:** Wings allow him to fly at hundreds of miles per hour.

5. **Black Widow:** Gauntlets fire high-voltage bolts of electricity.

6. **Thor:** Wields the mystical Asgardian hammer Mjolnir.

7. **Sunspot:** Absorbs solar energy to enhance strength and can fly.

8. **Iron Man:** Wears an armored battlesuit.

RECRUITING DRIVE

Early in their history, the Avengers tried to recruit Spider-Man as a new member. As part of the initiation test they asked Spidey to capture the Hulk! Spider-Man refused membership at the time, but continued to work with the Avengers on a reserve basis for years.

The Avengers excel at stealth, combat, and tactics.

BEETLE ABNER JENKINS

Mechanical genius Abner Jenkins built a flying suit of armor and became the costumed criminal Beetle. He clashed with Spider-Man several times before masquerading as a hero in the Thunderbolts team—and discovering that he actually preferred being good. Abner took the identity of MACH-1, leaving others to carry on the legacy of the Beetle.

The Beetle is constantly upgrading his suit to put himself in a better position for fighting super-powered foes.

VITAL STATS
REAL NAME: Abner Ronald "Abe" Jenkins
OCCUPATION: Adventurer; former mechanic, pilot, and professional criminal
BASE: New York City
HEIGHT: 5 ft 11 in (1.8 m)
WEIGHT: 175 lbs (61 kg)
EYES: Brown
HAIR: Brown
ORIGIN: Human
POWERS: Beetle's battle armor gives him the powers of a jet fighter. It has an arsenal of weaponry, grants him superhuman strength and durability, and its winged, jet powered harness allows him to fly.

The Beetle armor contains stolen Stark Industries technology.

SKY HIGH
Before he launched his criminal career, Abner Jenkins worked as an aircraft mechanic. He put his aviation knowledge to good use when designing his flying suit, allowing the Beetle to run rings around nonairborne heroes like Spider-Man.

Armor is lightweight but also completely bulletproof.

POWER RANK	ENERGY PROJECTION	STRENGTH	DURABILITY	FIGHTING SKILL	INTELLIGENCE	SPEED
	6	4	6	4	4	

BEETLE

JANICE LINCOLN

Janice starts a relationship with Robbie Robertson's son Randy, much to the horror of the couple's feuding fathers.

It could be said that Janice Lincoln was born into villainy, as the daughter of the notorious mobster Tombstone. Her father has ambitions for Janice to make her fortune as a corrupt lawyer, but she can't resist stepping into the dangerous world of Super Villains, becoming the Beetle to take on a mission for Baron Zemo.

The Beetle Armor Mark IV is built by the Fixer from designs by Baron Zemo.

FEMALE SOLIDARITY
Janice Lincoln believes in equal opportunities for women in the male-dominated crime industry. She sets up the Syndicate, a group of female Super Villains, with the intention of closing the pay gap and recognizing the value of women's contributions in the field of evil.

The "smart armor" is flexible yet durable and is fitted with mini repulsors.

VITAL STATS
REAL NAME: Janice Lincoln
OCCUPATION: Mercenary
BASE: New York City
HEIGHT: 5 ft 7 in (1.7 m)
WEIGHT: 135 lbs (61 kg)
EYES: Brown
HAIR: Black
ORIGIN: Human
POWERS: When wearing the Beetle armor, Janice has enhanced durability, and can fly, wall-crawl, and project repulsor blasts.

ENERGY PROJECTION	STRENGTH	DURABILITY	FIGHTING SKILL	INTELLIGENCE	SPEED
4	3	4	3	3	3

POWER RANK

BEN REILLY

Created by the Jackal (Miles Warren) to be a perfect clone of Peter Parker, for a time Ben Reilly believes himself to be the real Parker. When he discovers the truth he leaves New York, taking only the names of Parker's Uncle Ben and Aunt May, formerly May Reilly, to remember the past he thought was his. Later returning, he fights crime as the Scarlet Spider but has also had spells as Spider-Man.

As the new Jackal, planning to use cloning to end death, Ben Reilly chose a mask inspired by the Egyptian God of Life and Death Anubis.

VITAL STATS
REAL NAME: Benjamin Reilly
OCCUPATION: Super Hero
BASE: New York City
HEIGHT: 5 ft 10 in (1.78 m)
WEIGHT: 165 lbs (75 kg)
EYES: Hazel **HAIR:** Brown
ORIGIN: A clone of Peter Parker created by the Jackal (Miles Warren)
POWERS: Ben has Peter Parker's super-strength, speed, stamina, durability, agility, and reflexes, ability to wall-crawl, and spider-sense.

Sometimes Ben's skin shows signs of the degeneration that clones can be vulnerable to.

LIFE AND DEATH
Death herself tells Ben he has died more often than anyone in the universe, having been cruelly killed and resurrected dozens of times by the Jackal as he tried to build a clone without defects. These multiple traumas have a very detrimental effect on Ben's psyche, as does uncertainty over the validity of his identity—something felt by many clones.

As a clone, Ben does not set off Peter Parker's spider-sense.

POWER RANK	ENERGY PROJECTION	STRENGTH	DURABILITY	FIGHTING SKILL	INTELLIGENCE	SPEED
	1	4	3	4	4	3

BETTY BRANT

Her history with Spider-Man has often put Betty in the line of fire, but close encounters with Super Villains have also made her stronger.

As personal assistant to *The Daily Bugle* editor J. Jonah Jameson, Betty Brant spent a lot of time with Peter Parker. This closeness led to a brief romance, until Betty thought that Peter liked Liz Allen better. Betty became an investigative reporter, and is still one of Peter's closest friends.

Betty has a photographic memory, very useful for an investigative journalist.

PUTTING THE PAST BEHIND HER
Betty dated *The Daily Bugle* reporter Ned Leeds, and the two eventually married. Their rocky marriage ended when Ned was seemingly murdered by criminals, and many wrongly believed that Ned had been the criminal Hobgoblin. Afterward, Betty threw herself into her work, becoming a skilled and respected investigative journalist.

Betty's brother Bennett was the villain Crime-Master.

VITAL STATS
REAL NAME: Elizabeth "Betty" Brant
OCCUPATION: Investigative reporter; former personal assistant
BASE: New York City
HEIGHT: 5 ft 7 in (1.7 m)
WEIGHT: 125 lbs (56.7 kg)
EYES: Brown
HAIR: Brown
ORIGIN: Human
POWERS: Betty is an excellent journalist; one of *The Daily Bugle*'s finest. She is also skilled at various martial arts.

ENERGY PROJECTION	STRENGTH	DURABILITY	FIGHTING SKILL	INTELLIGENCE	SPEED
1	2	2	3	2	2

POWER RANK

BLACK CAT

Black Cat used to be a professional cat burglar, and she still has a wild side. She and Spider-Man once dated, which inspired her to become a more heroic person. Since then, her acrobatic skills have made Black Cat a valuable member of hero teams. She knows the secret of Peter Parker's dual identity, but he trusts her completely.

Despite their friendship, Spider-Man and the Black Cat have often found themselves on opposite sides.

VITAL STATS
REAL NAME: Felicia Sara Hardy
OCCUPATION: Adventurer, cat burglar
BASE: New York City
HEIGHT: 5 ft 10 in (1.78 m)
WEIGHT: 120 lbs (54.43 kg)
EYES: Green
HAIR: Platinum blond
ORIGIN: Human mutate; luck-based powers come from cybernetic enhancement with a quantum probability pulsator
POWERS: Black Cat has various devices in her costume that give her extra strength, speed, and agility. Her gloves have retractable claws, and she is an Olympic level athlete and martial artist. Her presence influences the luck of those around her.

Black Cat loves the finer things in life: her favorite drink is champagne.

A TRICKY GIFT
The Black Cat possesses the ability to manipulate the probability field in her immediate surroundings, bringing cases of inexplicable "bad luck" on her friends and enemies alike. With practice, she has learned to use this field as a weapon.

The Black Cat's costume contains various eavesdropping devices.

POWER RANK	ENERGY PROJECTION	STRENGTH	DURABILITY	FIGHTING SKILL	INTELLIGENCE	SPEED
	3	4	2	3	2	3

BLACK WIDOW

Black Widow uses all her intelligence-gathering nous and her fighting skills when she teams up with Spider-Man (Peter Parker) and Silver Sable to defeat the Sinister Six.

The Black Widow is a super-spy, trained to be one of the world's best secret agents. Her former Soviet masters shaped her from childhood to be a living weapon for their cause, but Natasha's willpower was greater than their brainwashing and she is now a warrior for good. During her long career she has been a valuable ally of both Peter Parker and Miles Morales.

ULTIMATE SACRIFICE
After Spider-Man (Miles Morales) was prophesied to one day kill Captain America, Black Widow stopped at nothing to prevent Miles from taking on that burden. Eventually she sacrificed her own life to protect Spider-Man's future.

Natasha wears wrist gauntlets equipped with her "Widow's Bite," an extremely powerful electroshock weapon.

Black Widow returned from the dead with her original personality put into a cloned body.

VITAL STATS
REAL NAME: Natalia "Natasha" Romanoff
OCCUPATION: Secret agent
BASE: Mobile
HEIGHT: 5 ft 7 in (1.7 m)
WEIGHT: 131 lbs (59 kg)
EYES: Blue **HAIR:** Auburn
ORIGIN: Human mutate; given Super-Soldier serum and trained in the Red Room to be a super-spy for communist Russia, but defected to the West
POWERS: Black Widow has superhuman durability and slowed aging. She is a superlative hand-to-hand fighter, master assassin, expert gymnast, and acrobat.

ENERGY PROJECTION	STRENGTH	DURABILITY	FIGHTING SKILL	INTELLIGENCE	SPEED
3	3	3		3	2

POWER RANK

BOOMERANG

Fred Myers moved from Australia to America as a small child. He used his skills as a baseball pitcher to become an assassin-for-hire, and tried to kill Spider-Man to win favor with the crime lord Kingpin. Later he joined the Sinister Syndicate to fight the wall-crawler. However, when Boomerang became Peter Parker's roommate and also worked with Spider-Man, the pair were shocked by how well they got along with each other.

Boomerang later sacrificed himself to save Spider-Man's life, protecting him from the vampiric villain Morlun.

VITAL STATS
REAL NAME: Frederick "Fred" Myers
OCCUPATION: Adventurer, vigilante; former professional criminal
BASE: New York City
HEIGHT: 5 ft 11 in (1.8 m)
WEIGHT: 175 lbs (79.38 kg)
EYES: Brown
HAIR: Brown
ORIGIN: Human
POWERS: Boomerang is an expert with a variety of boomerangs that contain explosives ("shatterangs") or gas ("gasarangs"), or have razor sharp edges ("razorangs").

His weapons always come back to him, but Boomerang keeps spares on his costume just in case.

SELLING HIS SKILLS
Originally recruited by a secret society to serve as their armed agent, Boomerang later pursued a freelance criminal career. With a deadly aim and an arsenal of throwing weapons, Boomerang has had no trouble attracting paying clients.

Excellent agility compensates for a lack of super-powers.

POWER RANK	ENERGY PROJECTION	STRENGTH	DURABILITY	FIGHTING SKILL	INTELLIGENCE	SPEED
	6	2	5	4	3	3

CAPTAIN AMERICA

As Captain America, Steve Rogers is a living legend. During World War II he was given a special serum that transformed him into a superhuman soldier. He fought the evil Nazi Red Skull, and after decades frozen in suspended animation he became one of the founding members of the Avengers.

In every grouping of the Avengers, including the one to which Spider-Man belongs, Captain America is the team's heart and soul.

VITAL STATS
REAL NAME: Steven "Steve" Rogers
OCCUPATION: Adventurer; former soldier
BASE: Avengers Mountain, North Pole
HEIGHT: 6 ft 2 in (1.88 m)
WEIGHT: 240 lbs (108.86 kg)
EYES: Blue **HAIR:** Blond
ORIGIN: Human mutate; enhanced to the peak of human capability by a Super-Soldier serum
POWERS: With his body honed to physical perfection by the Super-Soldier serum, Captain America is a superb gymnast, an expert military strategist, and a martial arts master.

CAP AND SPIDEY
Captain America is a veteran with decades of experience as a hero, but he has often expressed his respect for the much younger Spider-Man. Cap and Spidey have served together with the New Avengers, and teamed up to defeat the villain known as Queen.

Cap's indestructible vibranium shield doubles as a throwing weapon.

ENERGY PROJECTION	STRENGTH	DURABILITY	FIGHTING SKILL	INTELLIGENCE	SPEED	POWER RANK
1	3	3	6	3	2	

Carol Danvers is an exceptional hero with a wide range of talents. Formerly a spy, Air Force pilot, NASA employee, and journalist, Danvers is also—unbeknownst to her for many years—part Kree, a warlike and powerful alien race. When her Kree powers are unlocked in an accident, Danvers becomes a powerful hero, first as Ms. Marvel and later as Captain Marvel, taking on the mantle of her former mentor Mar-Vell.

Carol Danvers has always striven to be the best in everything she does, and when she identifies magic as one of her weaknesses, she goes all out to try to learn the art of sorcery.

VITAL STATS

REAL NAME: Carol Danvers
OCCUPATION: Super Hero
BASE: Avengers Mountain
HEIGHT: 5 ft 11 in (1.8 m)
WEIGHT: 165 lbs (75 kg)
EYES: Blue
HAIR: Blond
ORIGIN: Human/alien hybrid; born to one human and one Kree parent, Carol Danvers has latent Kree powers that are awakened when she falls into a machine built by Kree scientists
POWERS: Carol has superhuman durability, strength, stamina, agility, and speed; she can fire powerful energy blasts and fly.

BATTLING IRON MAN
Captain Marvel found herself clashing with Iron Man over whether to use the apparent ability of Ulysses Cain to see the future—Cain had foreseen that Spider-Man (Miles Morales) would kill Captain America, and Captain Marvel believed that Miles should be taken into custody preemptively to stop this potential tragedy.

She has worn many costumes over the years, but Captain Marvel's most iconic look is the red and blue suit, with a red sash to echo her earlier look as Ms. Marvel.

One of Captain Marvel's most important powers is her ability to absorb energy and then use it to fire powerful blasts.

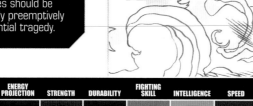

POWER RANK

ENERGY PROJECTION	STRENGTH	DURABILITY	FIGHTING SKILL	INTELLIGENCE	SPEED
-	5	5	4	3	6

CARDIAC

Spider-Man doesn't kill criminals, and tries to stop vigilantes like Cardiac who don't share his outlook.

Dr. Elias Wirtham became the vigilante Cardiac after a medical tragedy led to his brother's death. Transforming his body with cybernetic surgery, Cardiac set out to punish those he blamed. Cardiac considers himself a hero, but he often finds Spider-Man standing in the way of his ruthless revenge plots.

Vibranium suit absorbs impacts.

VITAL STATS
REAL NAME: Elias "Eli" Wirtham
OCCUPATION: Adventurer, vigilante, physician, surgeon,
BASE: Blessing Private Hospital, New York City
HEIGHT: 6 ft 5 in (1.96 m)
WEIGHT: 300 lbs (138.08 kg)
EYES: Brown **HAIR:** Black
ORIGIN: Human cyborg
POWERS: Cardiac has superhuman strength, speed, and durability. He has bulletproof skin, and his heart is powered by a beta-particle reactor. He wields a staff that projects beta-particle blasts.

WAR OF IDEALS
Cardiac's crusade has put him up against villains and heroes alike. He stole a device to help a girl with brain damage, forcing him into conflict with Doctor Octopus, who had taken on the role of Spider-Man. Luckily, Cardiac was able to convince Doc Ock to perform the surgery that saved the girl's life.

ENERGY PROJECTION	STRENGTH	DURABILITY	FIGHTING SKILL	INTELLIGENCE	SPEED	POWER RANK
3	4	4	3		2	

CARLIE COOPER

A forensic detective with the New York City Police Department, Carlie Cooper is the childhood friend of Lily Hollister (alias Menace) and a former girlfriend of Peter Parker's. When Spider-Man was framed for murder, Carlie used her skills to clear his name. She was also one of the first people to deduce that Doctor Octopus was occupying Peter Parker's body as the Superior Spider-Man.

Peter and Carlie dated, but she felt betrayed after discovering the secrets Peter had kept from her for months.

VITAL STATS

REAL NAME: Carlie Ellen Cooper
OCCUPATION: Forensic specialist; former criminal
BASE: New York City
HEIGHT: 5 ft 8 in (1.73 m)
WEIGHT: 134 lbs (60.78 kg)
EYES: Blue
HAIR: Brown
ORIGIN: Human; formerly enhanced via the Goblin Formula
POWERS: Carlie does not possess any super-powers, but she is a gifted forensic scientist and an expert in biology and technology.

Off duty, Carlie keeps a close-knit circle of friends.

When Carlie was forced to take Goblin serum she became the villain Monster, but she was later cured.

ONE TOUGH COP
Carlie is a reliable ally of Peter's and likes to unwind by skating with her roller derby team. Her detective skills are so strong that she managed to deduce Peter's secret identity as Spider-Man, temporarily driving a wedge between the two friends.

Carlie is an expert on Spider-Man's technology, including his web-shooters and spider-tracers.

	ENERGY PROJECTION	STRENGTH	DURABILITY	FIGHTING SKILL	INTELLIGENCE	SPEED
POWER RANK	1	2	2	2	4	2

CARNAGE

Crimson-colored alien symbiote Carnage chose murderer Cletus Kasady as its human host, resulting in a truly monstrous Super Villain. Carnage is so powerful that Spider-Man needs help from other heroes to defeat it. The symbiote has bonded with other hosts, but always returns to Cletus to continue its horrific rampage.

Carnage uses its body's sharp tendrils as weapons to ensnare its enemies.

RELENTLESS
Carnage is the most dangerous of all the alien symbiotes. It has no regard for human life and chose a relentless killer as its host. It is stronger than Spider-Man and its "parent" symbiote Venom combined. It craves chaos, destruction, and murder.

Symbiotic exterior can morph into different shapes.

Carnage has completely corrupted its human host.

VITAL STATS
REAL NAME: Cletus Kortland Kasady
OCCUPATION: Apostle of Knull
BASE: Symbiote Hive Mind
HEIGHT: 6 ft 1 in (1.85 m)
WEIGHT: 190 lbs (86.18 kg)
EYES: Green (white when bonded to symbiote)
HAIR: Red (none when bonded to symbiote)
ORIGIN: Human bonded with alien symbiote
POWERS: Carnage has superhuman strength, speed, and durability. It can generate swing-lines and vicious bladed weapons, and it can neutralize Spider-Man's spider-sense.

ENERGY PROJECTION	STRENGTH	DURABILITY	FIGHTING SKILL	INTELLIGENCE	SPEED
4	5	5	2	2	3

POWER RANK

CARRION

The original Carrion was a clone of Professor Miles Warren, alias the Jackal. Transformed by a genetic virus into a pale-skinned monster, this Carrion died trying to kill Spider-Man. Later, Peter Parker's university classmate Malcolm McBride fell victim to the same virus. As the new Carrion, he joined forces with the villains Carnage, Shriek, and Hobgoblin to go on a rampage across New York.

Spider-Man must be careful when battling Carrion, as his deadly touch could mean game over for the wall-crawler!

VITAL STATS

REAL NAME: Malcolm McBride
OCCUPATION: Empire State University science graduate student
BASE: New York City
HEIGHT: 5 ft 10 in (1.78 m)
WEIGHT: 175 lbs (79.38 kg)
EYES: Yellow
HAIR: White
ORIGIN: Human mutate; attacked by the Carrion virus
POWERS: Carrion's touch can disintegrate organic matter. He can teleport, levitate, and has telepathic powers. He also has superhuman strength and durability.

Pale skin is cold to the touch.

VIRUS EFFECTS
Carrion's abilities, including his eerie hovering and deadly touch, appear supernatural in origin. But like most of Spider-Man's enemies, Carrion's powers are science-based and began in a laboratory.

Carrion dresses in rags, as if he has just risen from the grave.

POWER RANK	ENERGY PROJECTION	STRENGTH	DURABILITY	FIGHTING SKILL	INTELLIGENCE	SPEED
	2	4	4	2	5	2

CHAMELEON

A solid punch can interrupt the Chameleon's concentration and make him drop his disguise.

Russian Dmitri Smerdyakov, alias the Chameleon, can copy anyone's appearance perfectly, and used his mimicry skills to become a spy for the Soviet Union. When Spider-Man foiled his plans, he became a criminal-for-hire. The Chameleon is the mastermind behind many of Spider-Man's trickiest cases.

FAMILY TIES
The Chameleon is related to the Kravinoff family, though he has no love for Kraven the Hunter or the other members of his clan. Nevertheless, he helped Kraven's wife Sasha Kravinoff organize the "Grim Hunt" that targeted Spider-Man and his friends for termination.

Chameleon's gadgets allow him to project holograms of his clothing.

An experimental serum makes his body completely malleable.

VITAL STATS
REAL NAME: Dmitri Nikolayevich "Anatoly" Smerdyakov
OCCUPATION: Professional criminal
BASE: Mobile
HEIGHT: Variable
WEIGHT: Variable
EYES: Variable
HAIR: Variable
ORIGIN: Human mutate; epidermis and skin pigmentation have been altered by a serum
POWERS: Chameleon's skin allows him to take on the appearance of any person at will. He is also a master of disguise, espionage, and explosives, and a crack shot. His computer belt allows him to instantly alter the appearance of his clothing.

ENERGY PROJECTION	STRENGTH	DURABILITY	FIGHTING SKILL	INTELLIGENCE	SPEED
1	2	2	2	3	2

POWER RANK

CHANCE

Bored with life as a professional gambler, Nicholas Powell became the mercenary Chance. Instead of charging a fee, Chance places a bet on his success—and pays his employer if he fails. Chance has learned that trying to kill Spider-Man is an expensive proposition!

Chance is willing to work with Super Heroes like Spider-Man, but he only really cares about himself.

VITAL STATS

REAL NAME: Nicholas Powell
OCCUPATION: Mercenary, assassin
BASE: The Palace, a penthouse in New York City
HEIGHT: 5 ft 11 in (1.8 m)
WEIGHT: 170 lbs (77.11 kg)
EYES: Brown
HAIR: Black
ORIGIN: Human
POWERS: Chance's armored costume has wrist-blasters and ankle jets for flight, plus various other weapons and gadgets.

Helmet allows 360-degree field of vision.

ROLLING THE DICE
Chance sometimes teams up with the web-slinger to capture dangerous foes. One such team-up saw him and Spider-Man turn the tables on the villainous Life Foundation when they tried to double-cross Chance. Spider-Man is grateful for Chance's help but doesn't consider him a true hero.

Backpack contains power cells to charge his wrist-blasters.

POWER RANK	ENERGY PROJECTION	STRENGTH	DURABILITY	FIGHTING SKILL	INTELLIGENCE	SPEED
	4	2	2	4	3	4

KEY MEMBERS

1. **Ms. Marvel (Kamala Khan):** Team leader Ms. Marvel can stretch or shrink her body and can assume any shape.

2. **Spider-Man (Miles Morales):** Spider-Man's unique power set makes him a key member of the Champions.

3. **Ironheart (Riri Williams):** Ironheart brings her elite tech and engineering skills to strengthen the team roster.

4. **Nova (Sam Alexander):** With amazing powers drawn from the Nova Force, Sam is one of the founding members of the team with Spider-Man and Ms. Marvel.

5. **Viv Vision:** The synthezoid Viv can phase through solid objects, fly, and absorb and manipulate solar energy.

CHAMPION

The Champions are a team of young Super Heroes who break away from their more experienced counterparts in the Avengers after becoming uncomfortable with the way their elders' personal differences could spill over into open conflict. The Champions want to help ordinary people and make the world a better place without any of the accompanying Super Hero drama.

The Champions travel to missions in the CMB—Champions' Mobile Bunker.

CHAMPIONS WORLDWIDE

Under Ms. Marvel's leadership, the Champions expand their roster to be truly global, enabling them to deploy teams across the world to fight multiple threats simultaneously. However, the team's growth is brought to an abrupt halt when a law is passed banning Super Hero activity for those aged under 21.

CLOAK AND DAGGER

Cloak and Dagger met as young runaways, teaming up for protection against harsh conditions on the streets of New York. Kidnapped and injected with an experimental drug, they gained powers—Cloak able to channel the Darkforce, and Dagger the Lightforce—and started trying to make the city safer. Perfectly balanced as a duo, Cloak and Dagger are always ready to help their friend Spider-Man.

The two heroes are dating and always look out for each other in times of trouble.

VITAL STATS (CLOAK)
REAL NAME: Tyrone Johnson
OCCUPATION: Vigilante
BASE: Hong Kong, China
HEIGHT: 5 ft 9 in (1.75 m)
WEIGHT: 155 lbs (70.31 kg)
EYES: Brown **HAIR:** Black
ORIGIN: Human mutate
POWERS: Cloak's body is a portal to the "Darkforce Dimension." He can teleport himself and others anywhere in the world,

VITAL STATS (DAGGER)
REAL NAME: Tandy Bowen
OCCUPATION: Vigilante
BASE: Hong Kong, China
HEIGHT: 5 ft 5 in (1.65 m)
WEIGHT: 115 lbs (52.16 kg)
EYES: Blue **HAIR:** Blond
ORIGIN: Human mutate
POWERS: Dagger can throw weapons of pure light.

Cloak can teleport himself and others, and also become ethereal.

FOREVER A TEAM
Cloak and Dagger teamed up with Spider-Man to halt the rampage of Carnage and his team of villains. For a time it appeared that Carnage's ally Shriek had killed Dagger, driving Cloak to despair, but Dagger returned even more powerful than before.

Dagger uses telekinesis to control her light blades and direct them at her targets.

POWER RANK

ENERGY PROJECTION	STRENGTH	DURABILITY	FIGHTING SKILL	INTELLIGENCE	SPEED
5	6	3	4	2	3

COLDHEART

Coldheart's specialized gear is government issue, but it has been tailored for her unique set of skills.

Government operative Coldheart turned rogue following the death of her son. Armed with twin swords that can freeze any target, she set out to take revenge on Spider-Man and Hobgoblin— those she blamed for the tragedy in her past. Imprisoned, she later broke out and went into hiding in Stamford, Connecticut, where she found herself at the center of tragic events that triggered the first Superhuman Civil War.

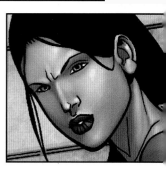

VITAL STATS
REAL NAME: Kateri Deseronto
OCCUPATION: Professional criminal; former government agent
BASE: New York City
HEIGHT: 5 ft 10 in (1.78 m)
WEIGHT: 140 lbs (63.5 kg)
EYES: Blue
HAIR: Black
ORIGIN: Human
POWERS: Coldheart's cryonic swords have the cryokinetic power to freeze or paralyze those she strikes, and project freezing energy. She is a skilled martial artist and swordswoman.

Coldheart usually wears armor in combat, but is ready to fight at any time.

EMOTIONAL RESCUE
Coldheart's training as a special agent made her more than capable of defeating Spider-Man. Luckily for the wall-crawler, she had a change of heart after she encountered a young boy who reminded her of her own child. Showing mercy, Coldheart retreated.

Coldheart's quickness with a blade is a challenge for Spidey.

ENERGY PROJECTION	STRENGTH	DURABILITY	FIGHTING SKILL	INTELLIGENCE	SPEED	POWER RANK
3	2	5	5	2	2	

DAILY BUGLE

The Daily Bugle published negative headlines about Spider-Man for years on the orders of editor-in-chief J. Jonah Jameson—even while Peter Parker worked there as a photographer! The New York City-based newspaper has seen many changes in ownership and journalism style over the years, at one point becoming tabloid *The DB!*, but it is now once again *The Daily Bugle* under the capable stewardship of Robbie Robertson.

KEY STAFF

Joe "Robbie" Robertson: Veteran reporter and newspaper editor.

Norah Winters: Investigative reporter who puts the story first.

Frederick Foswell: Reporter who lived a double life as Big Man.

Ben Urich: Hard-hitting journalist who battles corruption.

Phil Urich: Reporter who became the new Hobgoblin.

Spidey doesn't like the negative stories, but he's still a *Bugle* fan.

BUILDING A LEGACY
When wealthy media magnate Dexter Bennett purchased the paper, he briefly renamed it *The DB!* and focused on shallow celebrity gossip. The paper's reputation quickly declined, but Robbie Robertson has since vowed to make the rejuvenated *Daily Bugle* a world-class news operation both in print and online.

DAREDEVIL

When an accident involving radioactive chemicals blinded Matt Murdoch but boosted his remaining senses to superhuman levels, he became Daredevil—the man without fear! His father, a boxer, taught him how to fight, but Matt also studied law and defends the innocent as a trial lawyer.

Daredevil's identity as lawyer Matt Murdock is a well-kept secret, since few are aware of Daredevil's blindness.

Daredevil's trademarks include his horned mask and his "DD" insignia.

WATCHING FROM THE ROOFTOPS

Daredevil is the protector of Hell's Kitchen, a New York neighborhood on the west side of Manhattan. He frequently crosses paths with Spider-Man during their nightly patrols of the city, and they often team up.

Daredevil's now-famous red outfit replaced his original yellow costume.

VITAL STATS

REAL NAME: Matthew Michael "Matt" Murdock

OCCUPATION: Adventurer, vigilante, lawyer

BASE: Hells Kitchen, New York City

HEIGHT: 5 ft 11 in (1.8 m)

WEIGHT: 185 lbs (83.91 kg)

EYES: Blue **HAIR:** Red

ORIGIN: Human mutate; exposed to mutagenic chemicals in a traffic accident

POWERS: Daredevil has superhuman senses. He can detect lies, and is a superb detective, tracker, and martial artist. His cane converts into a club and contains a cable and hook for crossing rooftops.

ENERGY PROJECTION	STRENGTH	DURABILITY	FIGHTING SKILL	INTELLIGENCE	SPEED
4	3	2	5	3	2

POWER RANK

DARK AVENGERS

Norman Osborn used his political power to create a new team of Avengers under his personal control. Calling himself the Iron Patriot, Osborn recruited the Sentry and other villains to his team, including several hired to impersonate Ms. Marvel, Wolverine, and Spider-Man. Together, they became the Dark Avengers.

OSBORN'S DOWNFALL
Norman Osborn changed the lineup of his Dark Avengers over time. Eventually, he used his team to attack Thor's people during the Siege of Asgard. In the aftermath, Osborn was arrested and the original team of Dark Avengers disbanded.

KEY MEMBERS

1. **Iron Patriot:** Osborn wears a weaponized, armored battlesuit capable of flight.

2. **Ares:** As the God of War, Ares is incredibly strong and one of the best fighters in existence.

3. **Bullseye (as Hawkeye):** Can throw or shoot any projectile with perfect accuracy.

4. **Moonstone (as Ms. Marvel):** Has the powers of flight, intangibility, and shooting photon blasts.

5. **Daken (as Wolverine):** Has mutant healing factor and retractable metal claws.

6. **Sentry:** Possesses limitless powers of strength, speed, and molecular control.

7. **Noh-Varr:** Kree warrior with superhuman strength and agility. Can survive without air, food, or rest.

8. **Venom (as Spider-Man):** Has enhanced strength and durability, as well as the ability to shoot webs and scale walls.

Unlike its heroic namesake, Osborn's Avengers team consisted of hardened criminals, unstable villains, and ruthless mercenaries.

DEMOGOBLIN

When the Hobgoblin traded his soul for more power, a demon was bonded to him. Its supernatural abilities helped him to fight Spider-Man and Moon Knight, but the demon soon separated from its human host, and the Demogoblin was born! After the death of its first iteration, it was revived by Carnage in the body of Shriek (Frances Barrison), now calling itself Demagoblin to reflect its female identity.

The new Demagoblin entered into an infernal relationship with Carnage.

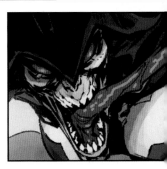

Demagoblin's agility, stamina, and strength are far beyond any human athlete's.

DEMONIC RETRIBUTION
Without a human host to guide it, the Demogoblin began its own demonic mission on Earth—waging war against sinners. In its eyes, that was almost everyone. Ultimately, however, the Demogoblin sacrificed itself to save an innocent child from a collapsing pile of rubble.

VITAL STATS
REAL NAME: Unknown
OCCUPATION: Demonic redeemer, cultist
BASE: New York City
HEIGHT: 6 ft 1 in (1.85 m)
WEIGHT: 210 lbs (95.25 kg)
EYES: Red
HAIR: None
ORIGIN: Demon
POWERS: Demogoblin's mystical powers created equipment similar to that of the the Green Goblin and Hobgoblin. It could fire heat blasts from its hands. In close combat, it used its sharp claws and teeth.

ENERGY PROJECTION	STRENGTH	DURABILITY	FIGHTING SKILL	INTELLIGENCE	SPEED
4	4	3	2	3	

POWER RANK

R DOOM

The supreme leader of Latveria, Doctor Doom schemes to conquer the world from behind an iron mask. He blames the Fantastic Four's Reed Richards for the accident that scarred his face, and uses his genius-level intellect to seek revenge on him and his allies, including Spider-Man. Although Spider-Man is often physically outmatched by Doom, he is clever enough to use the Latverian's gargantuan ego against him.

Doctor Doom does respect his foes. He considers Spider-Man one of his most worthy adversaries, though he can be angered by the wall-crawler's wisecracks.

VITAL STATS
REAL NAME: Victor Werner von Doom
OCCUPATION: Adventurer, scientist, monarch of Latveria, sorcerer
BASE: Latveria
HEIGHT: 6 ft 2 in (1.88 m)
WEIGHT: 225 lbs (102.06 kg)
EYES: Brown
HAIR: None (formerly brown)
ORIGIN: Human
POWERS: Doom is both a scientific genius and sorcerer. He can transfer his consciousness into another person. His battlesuit contains advanced weaponry and increases his physical abilities.

Doctor Doom's armor is made from titanium and uses nuclear energy to power its weapons systems.

DOOM VERSUS SPIDEY
In one of Spider-Man's earliest adventures, Doctor Doom tried to trick the wall-crawler into bringing down the Fantastic Four. His plan failed, so Doctor Doom tried to destroy Spider-Man instead. In a case of mistaken identity, Doom nearly killed Peter's high school classmate Flash Thompson.

POWER RANK	ENERGY PROJECTION	STRENGTH	DURABILITY	FIGHTING SKILL	INTELLIGENCE	SPEED
	6	4	4	4	6	5

DOCTOR OCTOPUS

His mechanical tentacles give Doctor Octopus the mobility and strength he would otherwise lack.

With four cybernetic arms and a brilliant brain, Dr. Otto Octavius has earned his title as the arch-enemy of Spider-Man. Doc Ock has tangled with Spider-Man in many different ways, from his creation of the Sinister Six to his romantic courtship of Peter Parker's Aunt May. He has even taken control of Peter's body and lived as Spider-Man.

Doc Ock's greatest weapon is his criminal intellect.

STARTING FROM SCRATCH
When Octavius realized he had only months to live, he transferred his mind into Peter Parker's body and started a new career as the Superior Spider-Man! But Peter's memories also showed Otto how to become a true hero.

Not particularly agile, Doc Ock uses his tentacles for fighting.

VITAL STATS
REAL NAME: Otto Gunther Octavius
OCCUPATION: Criminal mastermind
BASE: Mobile
HEIGHT: 5 ft 9 in (1.75 m)
WEIGHT: 245 lbs (111.13 kg)
EYES: Brown
HAIR: Brown
ORIGIN: Human mutate; bonded to experimental technology in a laboratory accident
POWERS: Scientific genius Doc Ock controls his four electrically powered tentacles with his mind. They can operate independently and are equipped with hugely powerful pincers.

ENERGY PROJECTION	STRENGTH	DURABILITY	FIGHTING SKILL	INTELLIGENCE	SPEED	POWER RANK
1	5	2	4	5	3	

DOCTOR STRANGE

Dr. Stephen Strange lost his ability to perform surgery after a car accident, but learned the mystic arts to become Earth's Sorcerer Supreme. Doctor Strange teamed up with the web-slinger to defeat Baron Mordo. He's been one of Spider-Man's closest advisors ever since, and also stepped in to help Peter overcome the villain Kindred by going to bargain with the demon Mephisto, Kindred's master, for Harry Osborn's soul.

As Spider-Man has a scientific background, Doctor Strange is a valuable ally when the web-swinger has to enter the realm of magic and sorcery.

VITAL STATS

REAL NAME: Stephen Vincent Strange
OCCUPATION: Sorcerer Supreme
BASE: Sanctum Sanctorum, 177A Bleecker Street, New York City
HEIGHT: 6 ft 2 in (1.88 m)
WEIGHT: 180 lbs (81.65 kg)
EYES: Gray
HAIR: Black with white streaks
ORIGIN: Human magician
POWERS: The greatest magician on Earth, Doctor Strange can project his body on the astral plane, and communicate telepathically. His Cloak of Levitation enables him to fly.

Doctor Strange can fly using the Cloak of Levitation, given to him by the Ancient One.

The sash around his waist is enchanted and can increase its length by ten times.

EXPERT IN THE OCCULT
Even when he's not home, Doctor Strange is happy to appear in spirit form to answer questions whenever Peter Parker comes to call. Despite his immense skill with sorcery, Doctor Strange is the first to admit that even magic has its limits.

POWER RANK	ENERGY PROJECTION	STRENGTH	DURABILITY	FIGHTING SKILL	INTELLIGENCE	SPEED
		2	3		4	2

DOPPELGANGER

The Doppelganger was one of many twisted versions of Earth's heroes created by the powerful Magus. Modeled on Spider-Man, but even stronger and with four extra limbs, he was the only one of his kind to survive the Infinity War. Deadly but with extremely low intelligence, Doppelganger went on to be a powerful yet biddable minion for evil beings such as Carnage, Knull, and Demagoblin.

Doppelganger was part of Carnage's plot to take over a small American town—Doverton, Colorado. The creature managed to escape the explosion that was intended to wipe out the Carnage symbiotes.

Doppelganger has only three digits on each limb.

MOMMY DEAREST
Doppelganger briefly found a kind of mother figure in Shriek, the "wife" of Carnage. When Carnage attacked her, Doppelganger leaped to her defense, only to be hurled off a rooftop by Carnage to his apparent death. However, he would later return in a failed attempt to break Shriek out of an armored car.

VITAL STATS
REAL NAME: None
OCCUPATION: Predator
BASE: Mobile
HEIGHT: 6 ft 5 in (1.96 m)
WEIGHT: 230 lb (104 kg)
EYES: White
HAIR: None
ORIGIN: A "fractal" being from the Dimension of Manifestations, shaped to be a fearsome copy of Earth-616's Spider-Man
POWERS: Doppelganger has super-strength, speed, agility, durability, stamina, and reflexes. He can shoot razor-sharp webbing and has fangs, talons, and four additional arms.

Doppelganger's web is razor-sharp and can cut through Spider-Man's web easily.

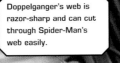

ENERGY PROJECTION	STRENGTH	DURABILITY	FIGHTING SKILL	INTELLIGENCE	SPEED	POWER RANK
1	5	5	3	1	4	

ELECTRO MAXWELL DILLON

While working as a power-service lineman, Maxwell Dillon gained electrical powers in an accident. He decided to turn to crime as Electro. One of the first Super Villains to go up against Spider-Man, Electro was a founding member of the Sinister Six and is one of Spidey's most frequent foes. After being killed by the new Electro (Francine Frye)—herself a clone after he had accidentally ended her life— Dillon was resurrected by Doctor Octopus.

Spidey's super-strength gives him some resistance to injury, but he has no defense against Electro's attacks.

VITAL STATS

REAL NAME: Maxwell "Max" Dillon

OCCUPATION: Professional criminal; former lineman

BASE: New York City

HEIGHT: 5 ft 11 in (1.8 m)

WEIGHT: 164 lbs (74.84 kg)

EYES: Blue

HAIR: Auburn (sometimes none)

ORIGIN: Human mutate; was struck by lightning while working on a powerline

POWERS: Electro can shape electricity into whips, tendrils, and nets. He can also fire electric bolts, travel along power lines, and control electronic machinery.

Electro's costume helps absorb damage.

CHARGED UP

Over time, Electro's powers have increased, and he can now black out the entire New York City power grid. He boosts his powers by drawing energy from electrical equipment, but risks being short-circuited by water.

Electrical bolts burst from hands.

POWER RANK

ENERGY PROJECTION	STRENGTH	DURABILITY	FIGHTING SKILL	INTELLIGENCE	SPEED
5	2	3	2	2	2

ELECTRO FRANCINE FRYE

Francine Frye idolized Super Villains and coveted their apparently thrilling lifestyles. It was this that led her to kiss Electro (Max Dillon), even though his powers were unstable at the time. A surge of electricity went through Francine's multiple facial piercings and killed her, to Dillon's horror. She was later cloned by the Jackal, and discovered that Electro's powers had transferred to her.

The new Electro shows her inexperience in her first fight with Spider-Man, allowing him to use water to defeat her easily.

Electro's costume is very similar to that of her predecessor, Max Dillon.

DEPENDENCY ISSUES
When Francine was first cloned, the Jackal (at that time Ben Reilly) had ensured that she was under his control by making her dependent on pills he provided to prevent her body degenerating. After his downfall, Francine's body stabilized and she no longer needed the meds.

Francine used to have dyed green hair, tattoos, and piercings, but these all vanished in the cloning process.

VITAL STATS
REAL NAME: Francine Frye
OCCUPATION: Super Villain
BASE: New York City
HEIGHT: 5 ft 8 in (1.73 m)
WEIGHT: 135 lbs (61 kg)
EYES: Blue
HAIR: Brown
ORIGIN: Human mutate; accidentally killed by the original Electro (Max Dillon) and resurrected as a clone with his powers
POWERS: Francine's powers are identical to Maxwell Dillon's: electrical energy generation and projection.

ENERGY PROJECTION	STRENGTH	DURABILITY	FIGHTING SKILL	INTELLIGENCE	SPEED
5	2	2	3	2	3

POWER RANK

EKIEL

The mysterious Ezekiel claimed that Spider-Man's powers were not caused by a radioactive spider bite, but were bestowed on him by the mystical totems of animal spirits. Ezekiel possessed spider-powers too, but he used his to become a wealthy corporate executive. Unbeknownst to Spider-Man, Ezekiel had another spider-powered being, Cindy Moon, locked away for her own protection. She was only discovered and released after Ezekiel's death.

Ezekiel usually dresses in a business suit, but goes barefoot for better contact when climbing walls.

VITAL STATS

REAL NAME: Ezekiel Sims
OCCUPATION: Businessman
BASE: New York City
HEIGHT: 6 ft (1.83 m)
WEIGHT: 180 lbs (81.65 kg)
EYES: Blue
HAIR: Gray
ORIGIN: Human who gained powers from spider-totem
POWERS: Ezekiel's abilities are similar to Spider-Man's. His spider-sense warns him of danger and he can cling to most surfaces.

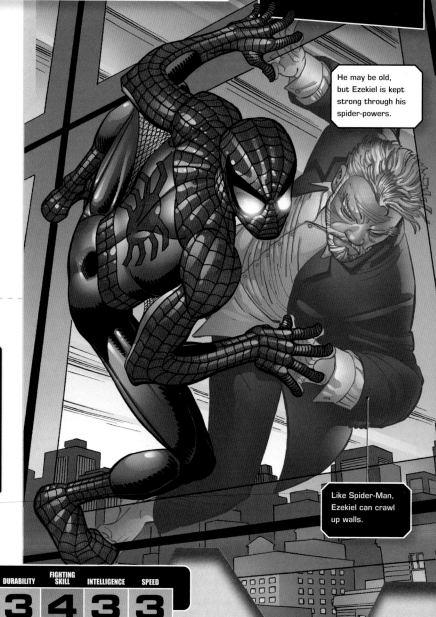

He may be old, but Ezekiel is kept strong through his spider-powers.

GUIDANCE OF AN EXPERT
After learning Spider-Man's identity, Ezekiel told Peter Parker that he could help him achieve his destiny as the bearer of the spider-totem. Together, the two defeated the ageless Morlun, a monster who fed on the life-force of the totem. Ezekiel later sacrificed himself to save Spider-Man.

Like Spider-Man, Ezekiel can crawl up walls.

POWER RANK	ENERGY PROJECTION	STRENGTH	DURABILITY	FIGHTING SKILL	INTELLIGENCE	SPEED
	1	4	3	4	3	3

The Human Torch is one of Spidey's closest friends.

FANTASTIC FOUR

The Fantastic Four are more like a family than a Super Hero team. They received super-powers in an outer-space accident and, as Mister Fantastic, the Invisible Woman, the Human Torch, and the Thing, fought evil from their HQ, the Baxter Building. Spidey joined them when the team became known as the Future Foundation.

Mr. Fantastic can stretch to unbelievable lengths.

KEY MEMBERS

1. **The Thing:** Super-strong and nearly indestructible in his rocky body.

2. **Mr. Fantastic:** Genius scientist who can stretch his body to incredible lengths.

3. **The Invisible Woman:** Able to turn invisible and project unbreakable force fields.

4. **The Human Torch:** Able to fly, cover his body in flames, and hurl firebolts.

PLANETARY DEFENDERS

The Fantastic Four are always at the front line when cosmic events threaten the Earth, whether it's an invasion from the Negative Zone or the arrival of an omnipotent alien Super Villain.

FIRESTAR

Angelica Jones is a mutant who can control microwave radiation. Friendly and outgoing, she has long been an ally of Spider-Man, teaming up with him and Iceman of the X-Men for a brief time. Firestar is very much a team player, and has worked with the New Warriors and the Avengers among others. She likes to work with other heroes, as alone she finds it hard to juggle the duties of being a hero with living an ordinary life.

Firestar treats her Super Hero teammates like family, and is fiercely loyal to those that she trusts.

VITAL STATS
REAL NAME: Angelica "Angel" Jones
OCCUPATION: Adventurer
BASE: Krakoa, Pacific Ocean
HEIGHT: 5 ft 8 in (1.73 m)
WEIGHT: 125 lbs (56.7 kg)
EYES: Green **HAIR:** Red
ORIGIN: Mutant
POWERS: Firestar has the mutant ability to project microwave energy and generate intense heat. Her microwave energies also enable her to fly.

AMAZING FRIEND
Firestar often pops up when Spider-Man needs assistance. Her positive attitude makes her an indispensable teammate with a knack of appearing in the right place at the right time. Active as a hero since the age of thirteen, Firestar is growing more powerful with every year.

Fire blasts are projected from hands.

Firestar's costume is immune to her heat powers.

POWER RANK	ENERGY PROJECTION	STRENGTH	DURABILITY	FIGHTING SKILL	INTELLIGENCE	SPEED
	5	2	2	3	2	3

FLASH THOMPS

Flash Thompson was the most popular student at Midtown High School, but used to bully Peter Parker. After Peter became Spider-Man, the two became friends. Flash lost his legs serving with the U.S. Army, but regained his mobility by becoming a new host for the Venom symbiote. He later became Agent Anti-Venom, and used his connection to the symbiotes to come back to life after being killed by the Red Goblin.

Flash served several tours of duty in the U.S. Army and won recognition for his bravery.

Flash considers himself Spider-Man's number one fan.

GROWING UP
As a teenager, Flash admired Spider-Man but hated "puny" Peter Parker. He later became a hero in his own right as a military-sanctioned operative armed with the powers of Venom.

Beneath his cocky exterior, Flash has the heart of a hero.

VITAL STATS
REAL NAME: Eugene "Flash" Thompson
OCCUPATION: Adventurer, black ops agent, vigilante
BASE: New York City
HEIGHT: 6 ft 1 in (1.24 m)
WEIGHT: 160 lbs (72.57 kg)
EYES: Blue **HAIR:** Blond
ORIGIN: Human bonded with symbiote
POWERS: The Anti-Venom symbiote grants Flash powers similar to Spider-Man's: superhuman strength, speed and agility, wall-crawling, and the ability to shoot a web-like substance.

ENERGY PROJECTION	STRENGTH	DURABILITY	FIGHTING SKILL	INTELLIGENCE	SPEED
1	2	2	3	2	1

POWER RANK

FRIGHTFUL FOUR

The Frightful Four set out to be a villainous version of the Fantastic Four. The team's lineup often changes, but evil genius the Wizard remains the leader. After many defeats by Super Heroes such as the Fantastic Four and Spider-Man, the team longs to come out on top.

KEY MEMBERS

1. **Wizard:** Scientific genius whose powered armor enables him to fly and to fire energy blasts.

2. **Sandman:** Has a body composed of sand that can be reshaped and change size.

3. **Trapster:** Outfitted with a variety of traps and glue-shooters.

4. **Medusa:** The royal Inhuman joined the Frightful Four after an accident left her with amnesia.

SPIDER IMPOSTER
One grouping of the Frightful Four decided that the best way to take down the Fantastic Four was by targeting Spider-Man! Trapster posed as the wall-crawler to sneak inside the Fantastic Four's headquarters, but the real Spider-Man helped stop the imposter and his teammates.

Like the Fantastic Four, the Frightful Four always comprises three males and a female member.

Wizard was offended when another villain team, the Fearsome Foursome, appeared to be ripping off his Frightful Four concept.

Fusion only appears to possess the weapons of Spider-Man's foes, but when he teamed up with Doc Ock the tentacles were for real!

FUSION

People are amazed when they see Fusion wielding the incredible powers of Thor or the Thing, but it isn't real. Fusion is merely spinning illusions. He first used his mutant powers of persuasion to get rich, but after his son died trying to imitate Spider-Man, Fusion launched a cruel vendetta against the web-slinger.

EVERY POWER UNDER THE SUN
Fusion burst onto the scene when he tried to rob a New York City bank, attracting the attention of Spider-Man. The illusions conjured up by Fusion included Captain America's shield, Wolverine's claws, and the mechanical tentacles of Doctor Octopus.

Weapons are mostly for show.

VITAL STATS
REAL NAME: Wayne Markley
OCCUPATION: Professional criminal
BASE: Mobile
HEIGHT: 6 ft (1.83 m)
WEIGHT: 190 lbs (86.18 kg)
EYES: Brown
HAIR: Brown
ORIGIN: Mutant
POWERS: Fusion's mutation allows him to manipulate other people's perceptions and create the illusion that he has various different super-powers. However, he does not actually possess these powers.

Fusion usually wears a black-and-gold suit, but he can alter it at will.

ENERGY PROJECTION	STRENGTH	DURABILITY	FIGHTING SKILL	INTELLIGENCE	SPEED
5	2	2	2	2	2

POWER RANK

GANKE LEE

Ganke Lee has been best friends with Miles Morales since kindergarten. The bond between them was so strong that Miles entrusted Ganke with his greatest secret—that he had spider-powers. After this, Ganke became his confidant and right-hand man in the world of super heroics. When his reality was destroyed by an Incursion, Ganke was one of the few people saved from that Earth by the Molecule Man and recreated in the 616 universe.

Ganke and Miles both attend the Brooklyn Visions Academy, where they room together.

VITAL STATS

REAL NAME: Ganke Lee
OCCUPATION: Student
BASE: Brooklyn, New York City
HEIGHT: 5 ft 6 in (1.68 m)
WEIGHT: 250 lbs (113 kg)
EYES: Brown **HAIR:** Black
ORIGIN: Human from Earth-1610, later recreated on Earth-616
POWERS: None

Ganke looks up to the mutant Goldballs as a plus-size hero.

Although Ganke is a totally loyal friend to Miles Morales, he has more than once accidentally told someone Miles' secret identity.

TECHNICAL SUPPORT
Ganke does not just provide emotional support for Spider-Man—he also supplies practical solutions to the problems of being a Super Hero. As well as helping Miles to figure out what the original source of his powers was, Ganke also uses his scientific smarts to make web-fluid for Spider-Man.

Ganke is a big fan of construction toys.

POWER RANK	ENERGY PROJECTION	STRENGTH	DURABILITY	FIGHTING SKILL	INTELLIGENCE	SPEED
	1	1	1	1	3	1

GEORGE STACY

Captain George Stacy of the NYPD was one of Spider-Man's most reliable supporters. He was a friend to Peter Parker too, having secretly discovered the truth about Peter's double identity. A hero to the end, he died while saving a child's life during a battle between Spider-Man and Doctor Octopus.

Spider-Man felt guilty for the events that led up to Captain Stacy's death, and vowed to do better.

Stacy had a reputation as one of the most incorruptible cops in the NYPD.

VITAL STATS

REAL NAME: George Stacy
OCCUPATION: Captain of New York City Police Department (retired)
BASE: Queens, New York City
HEIGHT: 6 ft 1 in (1.85 m)
WEIGHT: 195 lbs (86.18 kg)
EYES: Blue **HAIR:** White
ORIGIN: Human
POWERS: Stacy was an excellent detective and leader, trained in hand-to-hand combat techniques and the use of firearms.

A GOOD MAN

His sharp powers of observation allowed Captain Stacy to determine that Peter Parker wore Spider-Man's mask, but he kept the secret and only revealed it to Peter during his dying moments. His daughter Gwen blamed the death of her father on Spider-Man.

Captain Stacy projected an air of quiet competence, but he would leap into action when necessary.

ENERGY PROJECTION	STRENGTH	DURABILITY	FIGHTING SKILL	INTELLIGENCE	SPEED	POWER RANK
1	2	2	3	3	2	

HOST RIDER

After making a deal with the demon Mephisto, motorcycle stuntman Johnny Blaze is bonded to a Spirit of Vengeance to become Ghost Rider. With a burning skull for a head, he rides his Hell Cycle on a quest to hunt down evil. Blaze is not the only human to have been a Ghost Rider—other holders of the title have included Danny Ketch and Robbie Reyes, the latter of whom drives a Hell Charger car instead of a motorcycle.

After being killed by Mephisto, Johnny usurped Mephisto's throne and became the new King of Hell.

VITAL STATS

REAL NAME: Johnathon "Johnny" Blaze

OCCUPATION: King of Hell, stunt rider, adventurer

BASE: Mephisto's Realm, Hell

HEIGHT: 6 ft 2 in (1.88 m) (as Ghost Rider)

WEIGHT: 220 lbs (99.79 kg) (as Ghost Rider)

EYES: Blue (as Blaze); none (as Ghost Rider)

HAIR: Strawberry blond (as Blaze); none (as Ghost Rider)

ORIGIN: Human bonded with the demonic Spirit of Vengeance, Zarathos

POWERS: Ghost Rider's mystical motorcycle can drive up walls and he carries a heavy chain as a weapon. He also has superhuman strength and durability.

Ghost Rider's chain can be used as a whip.

Motorcycle leaves a fiery trail wherever it goes.

DEVILISH BARGAIN
The infernal powers wielded by Ghost Rider come from the demon Zarathos, a rival of Mephisto's in the spiritual underworld. Ghost Rider's human hosts must constantly struggle to stay in control, and take inspiration from heroes like Spider-Man.

POWER RANK	ENERGY PROJECTION	STRENGTH	DURABILITY	FIGHTING SKILL	INTELLIGENCE	SPEED
	4	4	5	2	2	2

GHOST-SPIDER

Teenager Gwen Stacy is bitten by a radioactive spider and develops a range of super-powers. When her nascent Super Hero career indirectly leads to the death of her friend Peter Parker, Gwen, or Ghost-Spider as she later becomes known, steps up her fight against crime in an attempt to assuage her guilt. She is a frequent traveler between realities, even enrolling in college in Earth-616.

Music is very important to Gwen, and she loves to let off steam by drumming with her band, the Mary Janes.

Gwen's costume is constructed by the Venom symbiote, which molds to appear like her old costume.

GWENOM
Ghost-Spider loses her powers when she is injected with a formula by Earth-65's evil Cindy Moon. However, she soon has the chance to regain what she has lost by bonding with her reality's version of the Venom symbiote. Although at first struggling with Venom's malign urges, Gwen learns to achieve balance and control.

Ghost-Spider's original web-shooters were built and gifted to her by retired Earth-65 Super Hero Janet van Dyne (Wasp).

VITAL STATS
REAL NAME: Gwen Stacy
OCCUPATION: Super Hero, musician, student
BASE: Queens, New York City, Earth-65
HEIGHT: 5 ft 5 in (1.65 m)
WEIGHT: 125 lbs (57 kg)
EYES: Blue
HAIR: Blond
ORIGIN: Human mutate; bitten by a genetically engineered radioactive spider to gain spider-powers; later loses those powers but regains them by bonding with a symbiote
POWERS: Gwen has super-strength, speed, durability, stamina, reflexes, and agility, as well as wall-crawling ability and spider-sense.

ENERGY PROJECTION	STRENGTH	DURABILITY	FIGHTING SKILL	INTELLIGENCE	SPEED
1	4	3	3	3	3

POWER RANK

GLORY GRANT

Glory Grant was working as a model when she moved into Peter Parker's apartment building. The two became friends, and Peter helped her land a job at *The Daily Bugle* as J. Jonah Jameson's assistant. Glory handled her boss's demands with ease, and transferred with him as his press secretary to City Hall when he became Mayor of New York City. She later returned to *The Bugle* as an editor.

As Peter Parker's new neighbor, Glory appreciated his photography expertise. She soon landed a job at *The Bugle*.

VITAL STATS
REAL NAME: Gloria "Glory" Grant
OCCUPATION: Editor; former assistant to J. Jonah Jameson
BASE: New York City
HEIGHT: 5 ft 8 in (1.73 m)
WEIGHT: 120 lbs (54.43 kg)
EYES: Brown
HAIR: Black
ORIGIN: Human
POWERS: Glory has excellent administrative, computer, and editorial skills, and is also an experienced scuba diver.

Glory has pursued careers in modeling and administration.

UPWARD MOBILITY
After J. Jonah Jameson was elected Mayor of New York City, Glory Grant signed on as his personal aide. In her new role, Glory is responsible for handling her boss's schedule and maintaining a friendly relationship with the press, including the reporters of *The Daily Bugle.*

J. Jonah Jameson respects Glory, though he rarely admits it.

POWER RANK	ENERGY PROJECTION	STRENGTH	DURABILITY	FIGHTING SKILL	INTELLIGENCE	SPEED
	1	1	1	1	3	1

GOBLIN KING

G

The nephew of *Daily Bugle* reporter Ben Urich, Phil interned at the paper for a while before acquiring Goblin powers. Although at first he tried to be a hero, he later fell into a life of crime and rose to be the Goblin King after the fall of Norman Osborn. However, his predecessor returned and, while merged with the Carnage symbiote, struck down the usurping Urich.

Urich possesses a sonic scream, also known as his "lunatic laugh," that is powerful enough to incapacitate Spider-Man and even bring down buildings.

Like other Goblins, the Goblin King rides a glider and carries a cache of various tricksy yet deadly weapons.

VITAL STATS

REAL NAME: Phil Urich
OCCUPATION: Reporter
BASE: New York City
HEIGHT: 5 ft 7 in (1.7 m)
WEIGHT: 144 lbs (64 kg)
EYES: Green
HAIR: Brown
ORIGIN: Human mutate; took Goblin serum after discovering a Green Goblin hideout
POWERS: Phil has super-strength, speed, stamina, durability, agility, and reflexes, and can emit a sonic scream.

Urich wields a flaming sword that he has carried since before he became Goblin King.

LOSING HIS WAY
When Phil Urich first acquired Goblin powers, he intended to use them for good as a new, heroic Green Goblin. However, whether because of the effects of the Goblin serum or some other trigger, he turned to villainy, running through various identities as the Hobgoblin, Goblin Knight, and finally Goblin King.

ENERGY PROJECTION	STRENGTH	DURABILITY	FIGHTING SKILL	INTELLIGENCE	SPEED	POWER RANK
2	4	5	2	2	3	

GOG

Reptilian alien Gog was just a baby when the spacecraft he was traveling in crashed in the dinosaur-infested jungles of the Savage Land. Kraven the Hunter found Gog and raised him to become his partner in a scheme to wrest control of the Savage Land from its protector, Ka-Zar. Spider-Man helped Ka-Zar to send both villains packing.

Spider-Man is really made to feel small by the gargantuan Gog whenever the two opponents battle.

STRANGER IN A STRANGE LAND

Gog is unable to speak any Earth languages. He can only make animal-like noises and form incomprehensible, alien words. Nevertheless, he is highly intelligent, able to operate futuristic technology and understand the commands of Kraven the Hunter and the other allies he has found on this strange new planet.

VITAL STATS

REAL NAME: Gog
OCCUPATION: Warrior, pet
BASE: New York City
HEIGHT: 300 ft (91.44 m) (variable)
WEIGHT: Variable
EYES: Yellow **HAIR:** Blond
ORIGIN: Alien (Tsiln)
POWERS: Pym particles in Gog's blood allow him to change size. He is super-strong and durable, and wears bracelets that allow him to teleport.

Gog is intelligent, but easily led by villains to serve their evil ends.

POWER RANK	ENERGY PROJECTION	STRENGTH	DURABILITY	FIGHTING SKILL	INTELLIGENCE	SPEED
	1	6	4	4	2	

GRAY GOBLIN

Norman Osborn's twin children, Sarah and Gabriel, believed Peter Parker was their father. Osborn told them that Peter rejected them after their mother, Gwen Stacy, died. When Gabriel discovered that Osborn was really their father, he blamed Spider-Man for Gwen's death, donning a version of the Green Goblin suit to become the Gray Goblin and attack Spidey.

When Gabriel Stacy attacked Spider-Man, the wall-crawler was reluctant to fight back for fear of hurting him.

Costume taken from one of the Green Goblin's secret weapons caches.

VITAL STATS
REAL NAME: Gabriel Stacy
OCCUPATION: Terrorist, Super Villain
BASE: Mobile
HEIGHT: 6 ft (1.83 m)
WEIGHT: 180 lbs (81.64 kg)
EYES: Brown **HAIR:** Auburn
ORIGIN: Human mutate; exposed to the Goblin serum
POWERS: The Goblin serum halts the rapid aging caused by Gabriel's Goblin blood. It also gives him superhuman strength, durability, and reflexes, and enhances his healing factor and intelligence.

A LIFE BUILT ON LIES
Gabriel injected himself with strength-enhancing Green Goblin serum and used the Gray Goblin identity to lash out at Spider-Man. Sarah halted a potentially fatal clash by shooting Gabriel's glider from under him. After crashing to earth, Gabriel was left with no memory of his brief Gray Goblin career.

ENERGY PROJECTION	STRENGTH	DURABILITY	FIGHTING SKILL	INTELLIGENCE	SPEED
1	4	4	3	4	3

POWER RANK

GREEN GOBLIN NORMAN OSBORN

A smoke-spewing glider and a crazed cackle are the Green Goblin's trademarks. In a quest for power, businessman Norman Osborn invented a serum that gave him incredible strength but cost him his sanity. As the Green Goblin, he terrorized the city during Spider-Man's early career. Eventually Osborn was returned to sanity with an antidote to the Goblin serum, but he came to conclude that his insanity had actually helped him in his battles against Spider-Man.

The jet-powered goblin glider can hover in place or reach extremely high speeds. It responds to remote control.

VITAL STATS

REAL NAME: Norman Virgil Osborn
OCCUPATION: Professional criminal mastermind
BASE: Mobile
HEIGHT: 5 ft 11 in (1.8 m)
WEIGHT: 185 lbs (83.91 kg)
EYES: Green   **HAIR** Auburn
ORIGIN: Human mutate; accidentally exposed to a chemical formula that increases strength and intelligence but caused mental instability
POWERS: The Goblin Formula gives Osborn superhuman physical abilities. His throwing weapons include pumpkin gas/smoke/explosive bombs. His tough Goblin armor includes gloves that fire electrical bolts.

Gas grenades are always kept within close reach.

Super-strength punches can stun Spidey.

THE DEATH OF GWEN STACY
The Green Goblin's most notorious crime was to throw Peter Parker's girlfriend, Gwen Stacy, from the top of a bridge. The Green Goblin seemingly died while fighting Spider-Man when his own goblin glider crashed into him. But this would not be the last that the world would hear of Norman Osborn.

POWER RANK	ENERGY PROJECTION	STRENGTH	DURABILITY	FIGHTING SKILL	INTELLIGENCE	SPEED
	3	4	4	3	4	3

The Goblin's smoke bombs sometimes included mind-altering gasses, giving the villain a sneaky edge over Spider-Man.

GREEN GOBLIN HA OS

Harry was devastated when he discovered that his father was the Green Goblin and he had died battling Spider-Man. Harry then found out that Spider-Man was his best friend, Peter Parker. Beside himself with grief, Harry became a new Green Goblin to get revenge. When his actions endangered the lives of his son Normie and Mary Jane Watson as well as Spider-Man, Harry rescued them, but lost his life in the process.

Harry's body reacted badly to the Green Goblin serum.

WHAT'S YOUR POISON?
Exposure to his father's strength serum gave Harry incredible abilities; in fact he became stronger and more intelligent than even his father had been as Green Goblin. However, the serum was slowly poisoning him and would eventually cause his death.

Harry both loves and hates his father—and the Green Goblin.

VITAL STATS
REAL NAMES: Harold Theopolis "Harry" Osborn
OCCUPATION: Businessman
BASE: New York City
HEIGHT: 5 ft 10 in (1.78 m)
WEIGHT: 170 lbs (77.11 kg)
EYES: Blue   **HAIR:** Brown
ORIGIN: Human mutate; exposed to the Goblin Formula
POWERS: Harry has superhuman abilities thanks to his father's Green Goblin serum; he uses Goblin equipment, including pumpkin bombs, razor-sharp bats, power-emitting gloves, and a glider.

ENERGY PROJECTION	STRENGTH	DURABILITY	FIGHTING SKILL	INTELLIGENCE	SPEED
3	4	4	2	5	3

POWER RANK

GRIM HUNTER

Vladimir Kravinoff blamed Spider-Man for the death of his father, Kraven the Hunter. Inspired by a hero from an ancestral legend, he became the Grim Hunter—and made Spidey his prey! After dying and being resurrected as a terrifying animalistic monster, Vladimir was killed a second time by his father so that his transformation would not bring mockery to the family name.

A ritual performed by his mother, Sasha, restored Vladimir Kravinoff to life as a lion-like predator, hungry for a piece of Spider-Man's hide.

In his new form, Vladimir is more animal than human, gnawing on bones and unable to speak.

Body is super strong due to his father's mystical serum.

HIS FATHER'S FOOTSTEPS

The Grim Hunter pursued both Spider-Man and his clone Ben Reilly (the Scarlet Spider) in his quest to restore his family's honor. He was killed by Kaine, another clone of Spider-Man, but returned to life through a mystic ritual, this time as a human-lion hybrid.

VITAL STATS

REAL NAME: Vladimir Sergeievich Kravinoff
OCCUPATION: Hunter
BASE: New York City
HEIGHT: 6 ft 4 in (1.93 m)
WEIGHT: 240 lbs (108.86 kg)
EYES: Brown **HAIR:** Black
ORIGIN: Human mutate; altered by the Calypso serum
POWERS: In his original form, Vladimir has superhuman physical abilities and fighting skills. He wears body armor, and wields wrist dart launchers and gauntlets that fire electrical shocks.

POWER RANK	ENERGY PROJECTION	STRENGTH	DURABILITY	FIGHTING SKILL	INTELLIGENCE	SPEED
	4	4	3	4	2	3

GRIZZLY

Maxwell Markham was a famous pro wrestler until an article in *The Daily Bugle* exposed him as a bully. Wearing a strength-enhancing exosuit given to him by the Jackal, he showed up at the newspaper's offices looking for payback. After repeatedly losing to Spidey, Grizzly teamed up with other villains, with little success. He has even tried becoming a hero!

Grizzly has sought to reinvent himself numerous times, but he has found it very difficult to escape the shadow of his criminal past.

Bear head does not restrict Grizzly's vision.

BARELY MAKING IT
Grizzly entered into a partnership with the Gibbon, but their efforts always ended in failure. The truth is, Grizzly values fame and fortune more than friendship. To make matters worse, his short temper makes him suddenly lash out—even at his own teammates.

Grizzly has sharp claws on his hands and feet.

VITAL STATS
REAL NAME: Maxwell Markham
OCCUPATION: Government agent; former professional wrestler, criminal
BASE: Miami, Florida
HEIGHT: 6 ft 9 in (2.06 m)
WEIGHT: 290 lbs (131.54 kg)
EYES: Blue **HAIR:** Blond
ORIGIN: Human mutate; has undergone a series of procedures to enhance his abilities
POWERS: Grizzly has a variety of superhuman abilities including increased strength and durability, and his fangs and claws can tear steel. He is also a skilled wrestler.

ENERGY PROJECTION	STRENGTH	DURABILITY	FIGHTING SKILL	INTELLIGENCE	SPEED	POWER RANK
1	4	5	3	2	2	

GWEN STACY

Gwen Stacy was a bright and popular student, first at Standard High, then Empire State University. Having lost her mother as a young child, Gwen was very close to her police chief father and loved to help him with his cases when she could. After meeting Peter Parker at Empire State University, Gwen became his first love. Her tragic death would later be one of Spider-Man's biggest regrets.

Spider-Man would always feel guilty for not preventing the tragic fates that befell Gwen and her father.

VITAL STATS
REAL NAME: Gwendolyne Maxine "Gwen" Stacy
OCCUPATION: Student, model
BASE: New York City
HEIGHT: 5 ft 7 in (1.7 m)
WEIGHT: 130 lbs (58.97 kg)
EYES: Blue
HAIR: Blond
ORIGIN: Human
POWERS: Gwen was a gifted biochemistry student and a curious, quick thinker. She was well-liked for her friendliness and generosity.

Gwen had a gift for investigation and sometimes helped her father with his cases.

One of Gwen's professors, Miles Warren, became obsessed with her, and as the Jackal created clones of her to torment Spider-Man.

LOST LOVE
When Gwen's father, Captain George Stacy, died during a battle between Spider-Man and Doctor Octopus, Gwen blamed the web-swinger for the tragedy. Peter wanted to tell Gwen the truth, but she died before Peter could reveal his identity to the woman he loved.

	ENERGY PROJECTION	STRENGTH	DURABILITY	FIGHTING SKILL	INTELLIGENCE	SPEED
POWER RANK	1	2	2	1	4	2

HAMMERHEAD

Hammerhead has gotten meaner and nastier over the years, and he takes it out on Spider-Man.

This flat-topped gangster earned his nickname after a brawl, when disgraced surgeon Jonas Harrow replaced his damaged skull with one made of steel. Hammerhead based his style on old gangster movies, and set out to clear the New York underworld of rivals, but usually found Spider-Man standing in his way.

Metal skull is his most powerful weapon.

EVEN TOUGHER
Hammerhead later received physical upgrades from Spider-Man's enemy Mr. Negative, in return for swearing total loyalty to him. He now has a skull and endoskeleton made of adamantium, a nearly indestructible metal.

VITAL STATS
REAL NAME: Joseph (last name is unknown)
OCCUPATION: Crime lord
BASE: Hammerhead's Mansion, Queens, New York City
HEIGHT: 5 ft 10 in (1.78 m)
WEIGHT: 265 lbs (120.2 kg)
EYES: Blue
HAIR: Black
ORIGIN: Human with a surgically replaced steel skull
POWERS: Hammerhead can smash through nearly anything if he charges at it headfirst. He has a keen criminal mind and is skilled with guns, especially machine guns.

Hammerhead is a skilled brawler, but prefers to use his head to tackle problems.

ENERGY PROJECTION	STRENGTH	DURABILITY	FIGHTING SKILL	INTELLIGENCE	SPEED
1	3	5	4	2	2

POWER RANK

HARRY OSBORN

The son of billionaire industrialist Norman Osborn, Harry Osborn became friends with Peter Parker when they were at Empire State University. Harry had a rocky relationship with his father, but when it seemed Norman had died battling Spider-Man, Harry became the second Green Goblin to avenge him. He would later try and make amends, rescuing his son Normie, Mary Jane Watson, and Spider-Man from a burning building, but died en route to the hospital afterward.

After he died, Harry's soul went to Hell, the price of a deal Norman Osborn made with Mephisto many years before.

VITAL STATS

REAL NAME: Harold Theopolis "Harry" Osborn
OCCUPATION: Businessman
BASE: New York City
HEIGHT: 5 ft 10 in (1.78 m)
WEIGHT: 170 lbs (77.11 kg)
EYES: Blue
HAIR: Brown
ORIGIN: Human
POWERS: Without the Green Goblin serum Harry has no super-powers, but he is highly intelligent and a skilled business leader.

As a failsafe against his death, Harry arranged for his consciousness to be uploaded into an Osborn AI along with that of his father.

HARRY RETURNS?

Sometime after his death, Harry apparently returned, free of the Goblin serum and ready to start a new life. However, it later transpired that this was a clone, and the real Harry was truly dead. The clone also sacrificed himself trying to save Spider-Man from Kindred.

Harry briefly became the armored hero American Son, as part of a sinister plot orchestrated by his father Norman.

POWER RANK	ENERGY PROJECTION	STRENGTH	DURABILITY	FIGHTING SKILL	INTELLIGENCE	SPEED
	1	2	2	2	3	2

HITMAN

Burt Kenyon once saved the life of Frank Castle (the Punisher) when they were in the U.S. Marines. After leaving the military, he pursued a violent path, becoming an assassin for the Maggia crime families. As Hitman he tried to take down Spider-Man, leading to a showdown atop the Statue of Liberty. Losing his life in this battle, Hitman later returned thanks to the Jackal's cloning activities.

Criminals lived in fear of heroes like Spider-Man, but knew they could hire the Hitman to keep their operations safe.

Military training gave Hitman an advantage in combat.

IN THE CLOUD
After returning as a clone, Hitman devised a way in which he need never die again. He uploaded his consciousness into a cloud so that it could be implanted into a new clone body whenever required. This gave him a tremendous advantage as an assassin, as he never needed to worry about escaping from the scene of a kill.

Hitman carried spare ammo in bandoliers.

VITAL STATS
REAL NAME: Burt Kenyon
OCCUPATION: Assassin; former U.S. Marine
BASE: Mobile
HEIGHT: 6 ft 1 in (1.85 m)
WEIGHT: 210 lbs (95.25 kg)
EYES: Brown
HAIR: Auburn
ORIGIN: Human
POWERS: Hitman is a superb marksman, hunter, and hand-to-hand fighter. His jet aircraft HQ contains high-tech equipment.

ENERGY PROJECTION	STRENGTH	DURABILITY	FIGHTING SKILL	INTELLIGENCE	SPEED
1	2	2	4	3	2

POWER RANK

HOBGOBLIN

Billionaire fashion designer Roderick Kingsley felt vulnerable after being attacked by a rival. Craving strength, he took Norman Osborn's Green Goblin serum, and became the evil Hobgoblin. Others have since followed in Roderick's footsteps, making the Hobgoblin a foe who has plagued Spider-Man at every turn.

An enemy of all spider-powered heroes, Hobgoblin goes after Spider-Woman (Jessica Drew) and those close to her.

VITAL STATS
REAL NAME: Roderick Kingsley
OCCUPATION: Fashion designer and CEO of Kingsley Ltd; former crime lord
BASE: New York City
HEIGHT: 5 ft 11 in (1.8 m)
WEIGHT: 185 lbs (83.91 kg)
EYES: Blue
HAIR: Blond
ORIGIN: Human mutate; enhanced via the Goblin serum
POWERS: The Green Goblin serum gives Hobgoblin superhuman abilities. He uses modified versions of Green Goblin's weapons and equipment, including Jack O'Lantern bombs, and a glider.

Pouches contain gas bombs and other explosives.

Flexible scale armor provides protection.

THE LATEST VILLAIN
Daily Bugle journalist Phil Urich later became the Hobgoblin. When his secret identity was made public he allied himself with the Green Goblin, pledging his services to further Osborn's crusade against Spider-Man.

POWER RANK	ENERGY PROJECTION	STRENGTH	DURABILITY	FIGHTING SKILL	INTELLIGENCE	SPEED
	3	4	3	2	4	3

HORIZON LABS

Horizon Labs was founded by Max Modell as a place where the world's best scientists could bring next-generation ideas to life. The team has also dealt with public emergencies, such as a city-wide outbreak of spider-virus. Peter Parker has been a Horizon Labs employee, inventing technology that benefits both Spider-Man and humankind.

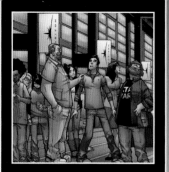

Impressed by Peter's scientific knowledge during a tour of the facility, Horizon Labs' chief, Max Modell, offered him a job on the spot.

HAZARDOUS SCIENCE
Horizon Labs is considered a menace by J. Jonah Jameson after he becomes Mayor of New York City. Although he knows its personnel are brilliant, their unauthorized experiments—such as a doorway that doubles as a portal through time—frequently violate the city's safety regulations.

Horizon Labs' headquarters was located at South Street Seaport, Manhattan, New York City.

When the South Street Seaport complex was destroyed, Max Modell relocated Horizon to a floating laboratory called *Zenith*.

With his battle cry "Hulk smash!," the Hulk is one of the strongest beings in existence. Gamma rays from an atom bomb test turned scientist Bruce Banner into the rampaging Hulk. He has switched between his two forms ever since—usually without his control. Spider-Man would rather help the Hulk, but sometimes he has to fight him!

Bruce Banner is a genius scientist whose suppressed emotions manifest themselves as different variations of the Hulk.

VITAL STATS

REAL NAME: Robert Bruce Banner

OCCUPATION: Nuclear physicist, Super Hero

BASE: New York City

HEIGHT: 8 ft (2.44 m)

WEIGHT: 1400 lbs (635.03 kg)

EYES: Green (as Hulk)

HAIR: Green (as Hulk)

ORIGIN: Human mutate; molecular structure was transformed due to gamma radiation

POWERS: The Hulk has almost limitless strength. He can leap several miles in a single bound and his body heals almost instantly.

Hulk has irradiated superhuman muscles.

AT WAR WITH HIMSELF

Bruce Banner tries to remain in control of his transformations, but outbursts of pain and rage often trigger the emergence of the Hulk. At times, Bruce has been able to keep his highly intelligent mind active within the Hulk's unstoppable body.

A stomp of Hulk's foot can cause a minor earthquake.

POWER RANK	ENERGY PROJECTION	STRENGTH	DURABILITY	FIGHTING SKILL	INTELLIGENCE	SPEED
	5			4	3	3

The acid Human Fly shoots from his mouth can dissolve various substances, including some metals.

HUMAN FLY

A crook who volunteered for an experiment to heal from a gunshot wound emerged as the Human Fly! The true extent of his powers emerged over time, and gradually transformed the Human Fly into a horrific monster. The Human Fly is easily one of Spider-Man's most disgusting foes.

High-speed flight is the Human Fly's greatest power.

The Human Fly chose a colorful costume to start his career as a Super Villain.

VITAL STATS

REAL NAME: Richard Deacon
OCCUPATION: Professional criminal
BASE: Mobile
HEIGHT: 5 ft 11 in (1.8 m)
WEIGHT: 200 lbs (90.72 kg)
EYES: Red
HAIR: Brown
ORIGIN: Human mutate; granted powers similar to those of a housefly by a scientist.
POWERS: The Human Fly has the powers of a human-sized housefly, with the ability to stick to walls, remain airborne with buzzing, razor-sharp wings, and spew acid from his mouth.

A DANGEROUS PEST

After gaining super-powers, the Human Fly didn't change his outlook. Sticking to crime, he clashed with various heroes including Spider-Man and Moon Knight. The Human Fly was apparently killed by an assassin, but underworld crime boss the Hood brought him back to life.

ENERGY PROJECTION	STRENGTH	DURABILITY	FIGHTING SKILL	INTELLIGENCE	SPEED
4	4	3	2	2	3

POWER RANK

71

HUMAN TORCH

Johnny Storm gained fire-controlling powers during the same cosmic accident that created the Fantastic Four. The most hot-headed member of the team, he likes to have fun and doesn't always take his responsibilities seriously. The Human Torch met Spider-Man when they were both teenagers, and despite some bickering they became good friends.

The Human Torch is flanked by his sister, Sue Storm Richards, and the Fantastic Four's leader Reed Richards.

VITAL STATS

REAL NAME: Jonathan Lowell Spencer "Johnny" Storm
OCCUPATION: Adventurer, firefighter, Chief Financial Officer of Fantastic Four, Inc.
BASE: New York City
HEIGHT: 5 ft 10 in (1.78 m)
WEIGHT: 170 lbs (77.11 kg)
EYES: Blue
HAIR: Blond
ORIGIN: Human mutate; exposed to cosmic radiation
POWERS: The Human Torch can control heat energy, cover his body with fiery plasma, fly, and fire a powerful "nova burst."

Johnny Storm cries "Flame on!" when turning into the Human Torch.

FIERY FRIEND
When they want to talk, Spider-Man and the Human Torch have a special meeting spot on top of the Statue of Liberty. During a time when the Human Torch was thought to be dead, Spider-Man took his place on the Fantastic Four.

When the Human Torch flies, he leaves flaming trails across the New York skyline.

POWER RANK	ENERGY PROJECTION	STRENGTH	DURABILITY	FIGHTING SKILL	INTELLIGENCE	SPEED
	5	2	2	3	2	5

HYDRO-MAN

Accidentally knocked overboard into an experimental generator, cargo ship crewman Morris Bench morphed into a being made entirely of water. As Hydro-Man, he signed on with the Frightful Four and the Sinister Syndicate to fight Spider-Man, and even merged with Sandman to create a rampaging Mud-Thing.

Hydro-Man attempted to submerge Spider-Man within the waters of his body, hoping to doom the web-slinger to a watery grave.

RUNNING WATER
Hydro-Man is difficult to damage, nearly impossible to contain, and can reconstitute himself from a single molecule. He has used his powers to travel through the New York City sewer system, searching for Spider-Man in order to set up an ambush.

Hydro-Man can convert any part of his body back to its liquid state at will.

Control over his molecules lets Hydro-Man take human form.

VITAL STATS
REAL NAME: Morris Bench
OCCUPATION: Professional criminal
BASE: Mobile
HEIGHT: 6 ft 2 in (1.88 m)
WEIGHT: 265 lbs (120.2 kg)
EYES: Brown **HAIR:** Brown
ORIGIN: Human mutate; knocked overboard by Spider-Man while an experimental generator was being lowered into the ocean for testing
POWERS: Hydro-Man can transform all or part of his body into a watery substance and emit powerful water blasts. He can also manipulate water outside his own body.

ENERGY PROJECTION	STRENGTH	DURABILITY	FIGHTING SKILL	INTELLIGENCE	SPEED
6	5	6	5	2	5

POWER RANK

MAN

Bobby Drake developed ice powers thanks to his mutant genetics, but he learned to control those powers as a founding member of the X-Men. After his body was possessed by fellow mutant Emma Frost, Iceman discovered that he had the potential to be far more powerful than he had previously thought. For a time, Spider-Man teamed up with Iceman and another young hero, Firestar, to form a crime-fighting trio.

Spider-Man and his amazing friends Iceman and Firestar battled villains as a super-team.

VITAL STATS

REAL NAME: Robert Louis "Bobby" Drake
OCCUPATION: Adventurer
BASE: Krakoa, Pacific Ocean
HEIGHT: 5 ft 8 in (1.73 m)
WEIGHT: 145 lbs (65.77 kg)
EYES: Blue
HAIR: Brown
ORIGIN: Mutant
POWERS: Iceman can freeze anything he touches and manipulate the water vapor in the air to form weapons from ice. He can race along on ice slides he creates for himself.

Bobby has come out as gay, and for a time was in a relationship with Emma Frost's brother Christian.

He can adopt an organic ice form, in which he is almost indestructible.

CHILLY RIVALRY
During one of their early encounters, Spider-Man and Iceman fought each other when Iceman believed that the wall-crawler had kidnapped an innocent woman. After working out their differences, the two heroes saved Robbie Robertson from a gang of thugs.

Iceman can also use his powers to create ice clones of himself.

POWER RANK	ENERGY PROJECTION	STRENGTH	DURABILITY	FIGHTING SKILL	INTELLIGENCE	SPEED
	5	3	4	4	2	3

1. **Morlun:** Has a special interest in Earth-616, having suffered rare defeats at the hands of its spider-powered heroes.

2. **Karn:** An outcast from the family since his failure to kill the Great Weaver cost the life of Solus' wife.

3. **Jennix:** The scientist of the group, Jennix is most content when experimenting in his lab.

4. **Daemos:** The largest of the Inheritors, Daemos is a formidable foe.

5. **Bora and Brix:** Twins, engaged in an ongoing competition over which of them can hunt the most spider-totems.

6. **Verna:** Favors hunting using her "hounds," savage beings she has captured and bent to her will.

The Inheritors are a family of hunters who feed on the life energies of beings who are links between the human and animal worlds—like those with spider-powers. They control the Web of Life and Destiny, giving them access to all possible realities and making them an existential threat to spider-powered beings everywhere.

The Inheritors' style of clothing reflects the fact that they have lived for many centuries.

MORTAL IMMORTALS
The Inheritors are immune to aging and disease and are extremely difficult to defeat, but even when death happens they are able to return via cloning, thanks to the advanced scientific skills of Jennix. This fallback solution is removed when the cloning facility is destroyed by members of the Spider-Army.

IRON MAN

Billionaire Tony Stark, alias Iron Man, is an engineering genius. After building his first suit of armor to escape from foreign captivity, Tony has designed many more Iron Man battlesuits for different missions. Iron Man is a founding member of the Avengers and a mentor to Spider-Man.

Tony Stark is one of the world's greatest inventors, and one of the few heroes whose civilian identity is more famous than his costumed alter-ego.

VITAL STATS

REAL NAME: Anthony Edward "Tony" Stark
OCCUPATION: Adventurer, inventor, engineer, CEO
BASE: Avengers Mountain, North Pole
HEIGHT: 6 ft 1 in (1.85 m)
WEIGHT: 225 lbs (102.06 kg)
EYES: Blue
HAIR: Black
ORIGIN: Human; formerly a cyborg
POWERS: Tony Stark's Iron Man armor gives him superhuman strength and durability. Jet-powered boots enable him to fly. His gauntlets fire repulsor beams and a chest uni-beam fires energy blasts.

A miniaturized reactor provides the suit's power source.

The Iron Man Mark 70 armor was intended to be a back-to-basics suit, although it still had an AI, named B.O.S.S.

MAKING MORE ARMOR
As a gift, Tony Stark provided Spider-Man with a new "spider armor" costume based on his previous Iron Man designs. Later, copies of the armored costume were provided to the members of the government-sponsored team known as the Scarlet Spiders.

POWER RANK

ENERGY PROJECTION	STRENGTH	DURABILITY	FIGHTING SKILL	INTELLIGENCE	SPEED
6	6	6	4	6	5

J. JONAH JAMESON J

When Jameson was elected as mayor, Spider-Man knew he would soon face more harassment than ever before.

Even Spider-Man's worst foes don't seem as dedicated to his downfall as J. Jonah Jameson. The former editor-in-chief of *The Daily Bugle* believes the wall-crawler is a public menace. For years, Jonah led a smear campaign against Spider-Man, unaware that Peter Parker worked for *The Bugle* as a photographer.

MISTER MAYOR
Believing himself to be the best man for the job, J. Jonah Jameson left *The Daily Bugle* to run for Mayor of New York City. He won, and one of his first acts was the creation of an "Anti-Spider Patrol" police task force.

J. Jonah Jameson thinks Spider-Man is a dangerous publicity-seeker.

J. J. Jameson leads by example, and was the hardest-working person at *The Daily Bugle*.

VITAL STATS
REAL NAME: John Jonah Jameson, Jr.
OCCUPATION: Radio announcer; former Mayor of New York City, Publisher of *The Daily Bugle*
BASE: TNM Main Office, New York City
HEIGHT: 5 ft 11 in (1.8 m)
WEIGHT: 181 lbs (82.1 kg)
EYES: Blue
HAIR: Black, gray at temples
ORIGIN: Human
POWERS: His forceful personality makes Jameson a formidable boss and a tenacious opponent. He is a master of media manipulation.

ENERGY PROJECTION	STRENGTH	DURABILITY	FIGHTING SKILL	INTELLIGENCE	SPEED
1	2	2	3	3	2

POWER RANK

J. JONAH JAMESON SR.

The father of the irascible *Daily Bugle* editor, J. Jonah "Jay" Jameson is a big admirer of Spider-Man, having been saved by him on his arrival in New York. That is not the only cause for conflict between father and son, as Jay Jameson walked out on his family when Jonah was still a boy. Jay comes to New York City to try and make amends with Jonah, and the two end up bonding.

When Jay met May Parker, the two embarked on a whirlwind romance and were soon married, making Peter Parker and J. Jonah Jameson family—albeit one that constantly bickered!

VITAL STATS
REAL NAME: John Jonah Jameson Sr.
OCCUPATION: Retired businessman
BASE: New York City
HEIGHT: 5 ft 8 in (1.73 m)
WEIGHT: 152 lbs (68.95 kg)
EYES: Brown
HAIR: White
ORIGIN: Human; father of J. Jonah Jameson Jr.
POWERS: Jay had no super-powers, but as a former U.S. soldier he had combat training.

Jay Jameson was formerly in the U.S. Army, and was deployed in the Korean War.

HARD CHOICES
When Jay Jameson fell critically ill, his family were offered the chance of a new treatment by New U Technologies. Peter Parker didn't trust the company, and he advised Jay to stick to proven methods. However, Jay died in hospital with his wife and son at his side. Although Jonah was angry with Peter at first over his father's death, he later realized that New U, secretly run by the Jackal, was dangerous.

He was very fond of his wife's nephew Peter Parker, and trusted him completely.

POWER RANK	ENERGY PROJECTION	STRENGTH	DURABILITY	FIGHTING SKILL	INTELLIGENCE	SPEED
	1	1	1	1	3	1

JACK O'LANTERN

Ex-CIA agent Jason Macendale became costumed mercenary Jack O'Lantern, with a flaming pumpkin head as his grotesque trademark. After Jason became the new Hobgoblin, the Jack O'Lantern alias was adopted by new bearers, including Steve Levins. Levins was able to return from the dead twice; once with the help of Lucifer, and a second time when he was cloned by the Jackal.

Spidey uses his webs to slow down the high-flying villain, but Jack O'Lantern is too well-trained to be led into an ambush.

KILLER CRIMINAL
The current Jack O'Lantern is a master assassin who uses weapons and vehicles that are similar to those of the Green Goblin. His advanced training and lack of mercy makes him even more lethal than previous incarnations of the villain.

Grenades can spray smoke or toxic gasses.

Gauntlets fire energy blasts.

VITAL STATS
REAL NAME: Steven Mark "Steve" Levens
OCCUPATION: Bounty hunter for Mephisto; former professional criminal
BASE: Mobile
HEIGHT: 6 ft (1.83 m)
WEIGHT: 200 lbs (90.72 kg)
EYES: Flames
HAIR: None
ORIGIN: Human who sold his soul to Mephisto for power
POWERS: Steve Levins can transform into a demon, granting himself superhuman strength, stamina, durability, and the ability to control fire.

ENERGY PROJECTION	STRENGTH	DURABILITY	FIGHTING SKILL	INTELLIGENCE	SPEED
3	2	3	3	2	2

POWER RANK

JACKAL

Biology professor Miles Warren perfected the forbidden science of human cloning. As he delved deeper into its mysteries, he lost his humanity and transformed himself into the Jackal. He created the horrific Carrion, the later-repentant Kaine, and the Peter Parker duplicate Ben Reilly (the Scarlet Spider).

The Jackal has known Peter Parker since his college days, and has knowledge of Spidey that other Super Villains would kill to possess.

VITAL STATS

REAL NAME: Miles Warren
OCCUPATION: Scientist; former biochemistry instructor
BASE: New York City
HEIGHT: 5 ft 10 in (1.78 m)
WEIGHT: 175 lbs (79.38 kg)
EYES: Green
HAIR: Gray (none as Jackal)
ORIGIN: Human mutate
POWERS: Jackal's scientific genius and knowledge of cloning has brought him superhuman strength. His claws are razor-sharp and tipped with poison; gas bombs are his favorite weapons.

Originally fully human, the Jackal has gradually transformed into his current state.

SCIENCE UNLEASHED

Though the Jackal is a brilliant geneticist, he is also a monstrous villain. In addition to his sinister cloning experiments, he caused an outbreak of spider-powers across New York by creating a virus carried by bedbugs. It infected every resident of Manhattan Island, unleashing mayhem on a vast scale.

POWER RANK	ENERGY PROJECTION	STRENGTH	DURABILITY	FIGHTING SKILL	INTELLIGENCE	SPEED
	1	4	3	3	4	2

JEAN DEWOLFF

Jean DeWolff always listened to Spider-Man, even when her colleagues wouldn't. After receiving a tip-off from the wall-crawler, Capt. DeWolff would lead a squad to investigate.

NYPD captain Jean DeWolff's love for the cars and clothes of the 1930s gave her a distinctive style. She broke ranks with her colleagues by declaring her support for Spider-Man. Sadly, she died when targeted by the Sin-Eater, leaving the wall-crawler with a heavy heart and one less friend in high places.

A LIFE OF SERVICE
Jean DeWolff's demanding father pushed her to join the police force. She was on track to become Police Commissioner, until the Sin-Eater cut her down in the prime of her career. Spider-Man and Daredevil teamed up to solve her murder.

Capt. DeWolff's no-nonsense attitude put her on the fast track to promotion.

Jean DeWolff had an eccentric love for classic fashions.

VITAL STATS
REAL NAME: Jean DeWolff
OCCUPATION: Captain of 37th Precinct, police officer
BASE: 37th Precinct, New York City
HEIGHT: 5 ft 8 in (1.73 m)
WEIGHT: 135 lbs (61.23 kg)
EYES: Blue
HAIR: Blond
ORIGIN: Human
POWERS: Captain DeWolff had police officer training, including crime scene investigation, unarmed combat, and the use of firearms.

ENERGY PROJECTION	STRENGTH	DURABILITY	FIGHTING SKILL	INTELLIGENCE	SPEED	POWER RANK
1	2	2	3	2	2	

 ## = MORALES

Jeff Davis was a former petty criminal who had turned away from that life to become an officer of the law, both for the NYPD and S.H.I.E.L.D. His marriage to Rio Morales gave him hope that he could be more than a thug, and the birth of their son Miles was further motivation to be better. When Jeff found out his son was a Super Hero, he did everything he could to support and protect him.

An encounter with Venom on Earth-1610 shattered Jefferson's family, but on Earth-616 all was restored.

VITAL STATS

REAL NAME: Jeff Morales (formerly Davis)
OCCUPATION: Police officer
BASE: Brooklyn, New York City
HEIGHT: 6 ft (1.83 m)
WEIGHT: 180 lbs (82 kg)
EYES: Brown **HAIR:** None
ORIGIN: Human, originally from Earth-1610
POWERS: Jeff has no super-powers, but is trained in armed and unarmed combat.

Back on Earth-1610, Jeff was seriously injured during when he was attacked by Venom.

Jeff was handpicked for S.H.I.E.L.D. training on Earth-1610 after Nick Fury observed his fighting skills.

SECRET LIFE
Jeff reluctantly agreed to rejoin S.H.I.E.L.D. after he realized that the organization could help him protect his son Miles. His marriage was put under strain when he decided to keep their double lives secret from his beloved wife Rio.

His main focus is protecting his family and setting a good example to his son.

POWER RANK	ENERGY PROJECTION	STRENGTH	DURABILITY	FIGHTING SKILL	INTELLIGENCE	SPEED
	1	2	1	3	2	1

JOHN JAMESON

Colonel John Jameson, test pilot and NASA astronaut, was a greater hero than Spider-Man—at least according to his father, *The Daily Bugle's* J. J. Jameson. John himself never made such claims, having a deep respect for the web-slinger. He remains a voice of reason between the two enemies.

John Jameson married She-Hulk at the Chapel of Love in Las Vegas, although their union was later annulled.

ALTERED ASTRONAUT
Exposure to outer-space artifacts led Jameson to experience a series of strange mutations. At first, he exhibited incredible strength—so much so that he was forced to wear a space suit to contain it. Later, in his most famous transformation, Jameson changed into the werewolf-like Man-Wolf.

In his Man-Wolf form, John's senses are superhumanly enhanced, and he can see in the dark.

Claws are so sharp that they can cut through wood and even some soft metals.

VITAL STATS
REAL NAME: John Jameson III
OCCUPATION: United States Air Force colonel
BASE: Mobile
HEIGHT: 6 ft 2 in (1.88 m)
WEIGHT: 200 lbs (90.72 kg)
EYES: Brown **HAIR:** Auburn
ORIGIN: Human mutate; contracted an extraterrestrial virus that transformed him into Man-Wolf.
POWERS: As Man-Wolf, Jameson has superhuman strength, speed, agility, stamina, and durability. He has acute senses, sharp teeth and claws, and can survive without air, food, sleep, or water.

ENERGY PROJECTION	STRENGTH	DURABILITY	FIGHTING SKILL	INTELLIGENCE	SPEED
1	2	2	3	3	2

POWER RANK

KAINE

Attempting a perfect clone of Peter Parker, the Jackal created the obsessed vigilante Kaine. This clone had a scarred face and the ability to give foes the "Mark of Kaine" with his burning touch. Though Kaine died in a plot by the heirs of Kraven the Hunter, he was revived by the Jackal. He would sacrifice himself again when he was hunted by the Inheritors, but returned once more to assist in their final defeat.

Kaine and Spider-Man haven't always gotten along. Far more troubled than Peter's other clone, Ben Reilly, Kaine has led a difficult life.

VITAL STATS

REAL NAME: Kaine Parker
OCCUPATION: Adventurer, vigilante
BASE: Mobile
HEIGHT: 6 ft 4 in (1.93 m)
WEIGHT: 250 lbs (113.4 kg)
EYES: Brown
HAIR: Brown
ORIGIN: Human mutate; clone of Peter Parker
POWERS: Kaine has Spider-Man's superhuman abilities, and channels burning energy through his hands. His spider-sense is imperfect, but allows him to glimpse the future.

Costume hides his identity.

A DESTINY OF HIS OWN
Kaine has made many attempts to emerge from the shadow of Peter Parker. After helping to end the spider-virus outbreak in New York City, Kaine relocated to Houston, Texas. There, for a brief time at least, he found his own identity as a Super Hero.

Kaine has enhanced wall-crawling powers.

POWER RANK	ENERGY PROJECTION	STRENGTH	DURABILITY	FIGHTING SKILL	INTELLIGENCE	SPEED
	1	4	3	4	4	3

KANGAROO

Brian Hibbs became the criminal known as Kangaroo, outfitting himself with an armored suit featuring a pouch-mounted cannon and a tail that could knock down walls. This Kangaroo found like-minded allies in the villains Spot, Grizzly, and the Gibbon.

Mysterio employed Brian and several other sometime villains as production crew on a movie he was making starring Mary Jane Watson.

Armor designed by villain named the Tinkerer.

NEW KANGAROO
The Kangaroo drew his inspiration from a previous villain, an Australian-born brawler (and possible latent mutant) also known as the Kangaroo. As the second Kangaroo, Hibbs uses mechanized weaponry to make up for his lack of super-powers.

Kangaroo's tail is dangerous to those who get too close.

VITAL STATS
REAL NAME: Brian Hibbs
OCCUPATION: Mercenary; former criminal
BASE: Australia
HEIGHT: Variable
WEIGHT: Variable
EYES: Brown
HAIR: Blond
ORIGIN: Human
POWERS: Kangaroo's armored suit gives him superhuman strength and amazing leaping abilities. It also includes a prehensile tail and a pouch cannon.

ENERGY PROJECTION	STRENGTH	DURABILITY	FIGHTING SKILL	INTELLIGENCE	SPEED
1	4	3	2	1	3

POWER RANK

Blamed for the death of his mother when he could not bring himself to kill the Master Weaver, Karn is cast out by his family, the Inheritors, for centuries. He is forced to wear a mask as a badge of shame, and is torn between trying to win back his father's favor and pursuing a less brutal path.

Karn renounces his family and chooses to fight against them on the side of the righteous— the Spider-Army.

VITAL STATS

REAL NAME: Karn
OCCUPATION: Former hunter; protector of Web of Life and Destiny
BASE: Loomworld, Earth-001
HEIGHT: 6 ft 2 in (1.88 m)
WEIGHT: 200 lbs (91 kg)
EYES: Red
HAIR: Brown
ORIGIN: Son of Solus and member of the Inheritors, a super-powered family who hunt animal-totems
POWERS: Karn has super-strength, speed, stamina, durability, agility, and reflexes. He is also immortal.

Karn's mask symbolizes his exile from the Inheritors.

He wields a two-pronged staff that can harness and redirect energy.

MASTER WEAVER
When Karn becomes the Master Weaver, his first call of duty is to repair the broken threads of the Web of Life and Destiny, destroyed by a rampaging Superior Spider-Man (Otto Octavius). However, his time as the protector of the web is brought to a violent end by his sister, Verna.

POWER RANK

ENERGY PROJECTION	STRENGTH	DURABILITY	FIGHTING SKILL	INTELLIGENCE	SPEED
3	4		4	2	2

KINDRED

As part of Mephisto's plan, for a time Kindred duped people into believing that Harry Osborn was the man behind the mask.

Gabriel and Sarah Stacy were originally created by an AI based on Harry Osborn, using DNA from his father, Norman, and Gwen Stacy. Later they were remade in Hell by Mephisto, who gave them demonic powers to create a new villain, Kindred. At first Kindred was believed to be just one being, sent to torment Spider-Man in a variety of ways as only Mephisto could.

The version of Kindred can be determined by the color of jacket it wears: brown for Gabriel Stacy, purple for Sarah.

Kindred is always seen accompanied by various invertebrates, especially centipedes.

VITAL STATS
REAL NAME: Gabriel and Sarah Stacy
OCCUPATION: Demon
BASE: Mobile
HEIGHT: Variable **WEIGHT:** Variable
EYES: Red **HAIR:** None
ORIGIN: Genetically engineered humans affected by the Goblin Formula; later given demonic powers by Mephisto
POWERS: Kindred's demonic powers including resurrecting the dead and being able to possess others. They also have super-strength and durability.

ANTI-AGING FORMULA
When the twins were created, the DNA from Norman Osborn's Goblin-Formula-enhanced blood had the unexpected side effect of causing them to age rapidly. They ended up in a cycle of death and recreation that was only broken when Mephisto stepped in—their demonic transformation into Kindred stopping the rapid aging.

ENERGY PROJECTION	STRENGTH	DURABILITY	FIGHTING SKILL	INTELLIGENCE	SPEED	POWER RANK
1	4	5	3	3	3	

KINGPIN

The boss of New York's crime scene, the Kingpin worked his way up the underworld ladder, eliminating rivals and making enemies of the Maggia crime syndicate. He suffered personal tragedy along the way when he lost his wife Vanessa and son Richard. The Kingpin is one of Spider-Man's most powerful enemies, and he has ruthlessly targeted those closest to Peter Parker, although he claims to respect him.

Even with Spidey's super-strength, it can be tough for him to get the upper hand on the Kingpin.

VITAL STATS
REAL NAME: Wilson Grant Fisk
OCCUPATION: Criminal mastermind; former Mayor of New York City
BASE: New York City
HEIGHT: 6 ft 7 in (2.01 m)
WEIGHT: 450 lbs (204.12 kg)
EYES: Blue
HAIR: None
ORIGIN: Human
POWERS: Kingpin has a brilliant criminal mind and formidable hand-to-hand combat skills. His huge body is almost solid muscle.

His bulk, often mistaken for fat, is pure muscle.

The Kingpin dresses in the finest suits money can buy.

UNTOUCHABLE
The Kingpin is prepared for anything, and can outwit almost any opponent. Spider-Man has been forced to back down from busting him in the past, after realizing that he didn't have enough evidence to send the crime boss to jail permanently.

POWER RANK	ENERGY PROJECTION	STRENGTH	DURABILITY	FIGHTING SKILL	INTELLIGENCE	SPEED
	1	3	2	5	3	

KRAVEN THE HUN

Sergei Kravinoff was determined to become the greatest hunter who ever lived. However, he knew he could never truly be the best if he couldn't defeat Spider-Man. Calling himself Kraven the Hunter, he relentlessly pursued the wall-crawler. After dying and being resurrected by his family, Kraven finds himself cursed with a form of immortality in which he can only be killed by Spider-Man.

Kraven often commands animals to do his bidding, including leopards, tigers, and other predatory cats.

Kraven's furred vest resembles the mane of a lion.

Kraven's strength has been boosted beyond human limits.

VITAL STATS

REAL NAME: Sergei Nikolaevich Kravinoff

OCCUPATION: Hunter, mercenary

BASE: Savage Land, Antarctica

HEIGHT: 6 ft (1.83 m)

WEIGHT: 235 lbs (106.59 kg)

EYES: Brown **HAIR:** Black

ORIGIN: Human mutate; augmented by mystical potions

POWERS: Kraven is an expert tracker and hunter. His strength and stamina are enhanced, and he has an extended life span.

AN ENDING AND A BEGINNING

In what he considered his "Last Hunt," Kraven finally beat Spider-Man and then took his own life. His wife Sasha Kravinoff gathered the family to hunt Spider-Man's allies and perform a mystic ritual to enable Kraven to return from the dead.

ENERGY PROJECTION	STRENGTH	DURABILITY	FIGHTING SKILL	INTELLIGENCE	SPEED	POWER RANK
1	4	3	6	3	3	

LADY OCTOPUS

The daughter of scientist Seward Trainer, Carolyn Trainer is taught that there is nothing more important than scientific research. Inheriting her father's aptitude but resenting him for his neglect, she gets a job as Doctor Octopus' lab assistant. When Doc Ock is killed, Carolyn takes over his tentacles and his identity, later becoming Lady Octopus when Octavius is revived.

Carolyn Trainer was handpicked by Doctor Octopus as a virtual reality expert. She used her advanced skills to create a copy of his mind, stored on computer files to be used in the event of anything happening to him.

VITAL STATS

REAL NAME: Carolyn Trainer
OCCUPATION: Super Villain
BASE: New York City
HEIGHT: 5 ft 10 in (1.78 m)
WEIGHT: 140 lbs (63.5 kg)
EYES: Brown
HAIR: Brown
ORIGIN: Human; acquired a set of robotic tentacles like those of Doctor Octopus
POWERS: Psionic control of metal tentacle harness, giving super-strength and speed plus force-field projection and the ability to interface with various external technologies.

Lady Octopus is extremely health-conscious and follows an organic, vegan diet.

EVIL GENIUS
Lady Octopus was raised to revere science and technology, devoting her life to the pursuit of excellence in various fields, especially computer science. She devised the theory of inherited clone memory and has multiple degrees. However, like Doctor Octopus before her, she uses her genius for evil.

Her tentacles have many functions and are controlled mentally; she can also generate a force field.

POWER RANK

ENERGY PROJECTION	STRENGTH	DURABILITY	FIGHTING SKILL	INTELLIGENCE	SPEED
3	3	4	3	5	4

LEAP-FROG

Failed inventor Vinnie Patilio turned to crime after discovering he could use electrical coils to jump over rooftops. Fashioning an amphibian-themed costume, he became Leap-Frog and battled Daredevil and Spider-Man. Leap-Frog isn't much of a threat, but he hopes to make it to the criminal big leagues someday.

To his credit, Leap-Frog never considered himself a threat on the level of Doctor Octopus. If Spider-Man shows up, he'd rather run than fight.

Electrical coils permit power-jumps.

Aging body is in poor condition.

IT RUNS IN THE FAMILY
Leap-Frog has a son, Frog-Man, who is one of Spider-Man's biggest fans. At the invitation of Frog-Man, Spider-Man spent an evening at the Patilio home. After dinner, both Leap-Frog and Frog-Man leaped into action to help the wall-crawler defeat the White Rabbit.

VITAL STATS
REAL NAME: Vincent Patilio
OCCUPATION: Inventor
BASE: New York City
HEIGHT: 5 ft 9 in (1.75 m)
WEIGHT: 170 lbs (77.11 kg)
EYES: Brown
HAIR: Brown
ORIGIN: Human
POWERS: Leap-Frog can make massive leaps owing to electrical coils in his boots. His suit's exoskeleton enhances his strength.

ENERGY PROJECTION	STRENGTH	DURABILITY	FIGHTING SKILL	INTELLIGENCE	SPEED
1	3	3	2	4	3

POWER RANK

LIGHTMASTER

Dismayed by budget cuts, physics professor Dr. Edward Lansky became Lightmaster. A special suit allowed him to absorb and emit photons, and he worked with Kraven the Hunter and Tarantula while extorting city officials into providing funding for university programs. Spider-Man thought he had ended Lightmaster's criminal campaign, but the villain got out of jail and returned to his old ways, joining a new version of the Masters of Evil.

Lightmaster was rescued by his daughter Selah (aka Sun Girl) after being wounded in a clash with the Superior Six.

VITAL STATS

REAL NAME: Edward Lansky
OCCUPATION: Former teacher and vice chancellor of Empire State University
BASE: New York City
HEIGHT: 5 ft 11 in (1.8 m)
WEIGHT: 175 lbs (79.38 kg)
EYES: Brown
HAIR: Brown
ORIGIN: Human mutate; transformed into a being made of light after an accident involving his suit
POWERS: Lightmaster can absorb or generate light, create solid objects from light, and fly. He is also immune to telepathy.

Containment suit enables absorption of electromagnetic energy.

Lightmaster uses his powers to fly.

LIGHTS OUT

An accident transformed Lightmaster into a being composed entirely of energy. He tried a number of schemes to regain his humanity but was eventually restored by the hero Quasar, working together with Spider-Man. Lightmaster has since returned to using a suit to gain his light-based powers, and a life of crime.

POWER RANK

ENERGY PROJECTION	STRENGTH	DURABILITY	FIGHTING SKILL	INTELLIGENCE	SPEED
6	2	2	2	5	6

LIVING BRAIN

The artificial intelligence of the Living Brain could deduce the answer to any question, including "Who is Spider-Man?" Luckily for Peter Parker, when the robot came to Midtown High School it went on a rampage before it could reveal its findings. It was later captured by the Superior Spider-Man (Otto Octavius) and reprogrammed to be a lab assistant at Parker Industries.

The original Living Brain, revolutionary for its time, has been upgraded over the years to keep pace with advances in processing power and artificial intelligence.

The Living Brain was rebuilt in its current form by Anna Maria Marconi.

Nanites stored inside the Living Brain allow it to repair itself.

VALUABLE HARDWARE
Since its first appearance at Midtown High School, the Living Brain has been upgraded with a speech synthesizer and an improved processor. It served as a member of the Sinister Six, using its advanced intelligence to calculate success probabilities and escape vectors, and Octavius also used it as a vessel for his consciousness after his death.

VITAL STATS
REAL NAME: None
OCCUPATION: Computer
BASE: Parker Industries, New York City
HEIGHT: 6 ft 6 in (1.98 m)
WEIGHT: 800 lbs (362.87 kg)
EYES: Yellow
HAIR: None
ORIGIN: Robot
POWERS: The Living Brain can outthink any human being and is incapable of forgetting anything. It fights by rapidly spinning its arms and body.

ENERGY PROJECTION	STRENGTH	DURABILITY	FIGHTING SKILL	INTELLIGENCE	SPEED	POWER RANK
1	5		4		4	

LIZ ALLAN

Liz Allan was one of the most popular students at Midtown High School, unlike shy Peter Parker. But Liz saw Peter's kind heart and became his close friend. She spent years caring for her stepbrother Mark Raxton, the Molten Man, and remains a key ally of Spider-Man.

The most important person in Liz Allan's life is her son, Normie. She hopes that he will take control of the Allan business enterprise when he is old enough.

VITAL STATS

REAL NAME:
Elizabeth "Liz" Allan

OCCUPATION: CEO of Alchemax

BASE: Alchemax Tower, New York City

HEIGHT: 5 ft 9 in (1.75 m)

WEIGHT: 135 lbs (61.23 kg)

EYES: Blue

HAIR: Blond

ORIGIN: Human

POWERS: Liz is a skilled corporate leader with experience in international business. Close encounters with Super Villains have left her with above-average fighting skills.

Liz Allan has achieved great success in the science and research industry.

FAMILY BUSINESS
Liz Allan married Harry Osborn, and had a son, Normie (named after Harry's father Norman Osborn). Accustomed to wealth and power, Liz ran the Osborn corporate empire for a time. She has since taken control of the family business, Allan Chemical, and merged it with Horizon Labs to create a powerful new company called Alchemax.

POWER RANK

ENERGY PROJECTION	STRENGTH	DURABILITY	FIGHTING SKILL	INTELLIGENCE	SPEED
1	2	2	2	2	2

When the Lizard's primal, reptilian brain is in control, Dr. Curt Connors can't recognize his friend Spider-Man or show him mercy.

LIZARD

Dr. Curt Connors' secret formula, based on reptile DNA, restored his missing arm, but also mutated him into his gruesome alter-ego, the Lizard! Spider-Man first faced the Lizard in the Florida Everglades, but the monster followed him to New York City for many more showdowns.

SUPPRESSING THE PREDATOR

Curt Connors is sometimes a friend to Spider-Man, but only when he is able to keep his animal side under control. The Lizard joined with Doctor Octopus to steal Lily Hollister's baby away from her, but when Curt Connors' good nature resurfaced, the Lizard handed the baby over to Spider-Man.

Thick, reptilian hide is difficult to damage.

Spidey and the Lizard have a long history, both in and out of costume.

VITAL STATS

REAL NAME:
Curtis "Curt" Connors
OCCUPATION: College professor, researcher in bio-genetics
BASE: Empire State University, New York City
HEIGHT: 5 ft 11 in (1.8 m) (Connors); 6 ft 8 in (2.03 m) (Lizard)
WEIGHT: 175 lbs (79.38 kg) (Connors); 550 lbs (249.48 kg) (Lizard)
EYES: Blue (red as Lizard)
HAIR: Brown (none as Lizard)
ORIGIN: Human mutate; transformed by the Connors Formula
POWERS: The Lizard can cling to walls and control reptiles telepathically. He also has superhuman strength and speed, and razor-sharp teeth.

ENERGY PROJECTION	STRENGTH	DURABILITY	FIGHTING SKILL	INTELLIGENCE	SPEED	POWER RANK
1	4	5	2	5	3	

LOOTER

Disgraced scientist Norton Fester finally got a lucky break when his examination of a meteorite released a cloud of strange gasses. Norton found that the gasses had honed his body to peak physical perfection, and he engaged in big-ticket robberies as the Looter. Luckily, Spider-Man is usually there to stop him.

More recently, the Looter has also gone by the alias of Meteor Man. He uses balloons to escape from the scenes of his crimes.

VITAL STATS

REAL NAME: Norton G. Fester
OCCUPATION: Professional criminal; former scientist
BASE: New York City
HEIGHT: 5 ft 9 in (1.75 m)
WEIGHT: 150 lbs (68.04 kg)
EYES: Brown
HAIR: Brown
ORIGIN: Human mutate; exposed to mysterious interstellar gasses
POWERS: Looter has superhuman strength, and can survive falls from great heights. He uses a variety of gadgets of his own invention, including a blinding dazzle gun.

True to his name, Looter uses equipment and weapons stolen from other villains.

SPECIAL TREASURES

The Looter needs special meteorites in order to maintain his physical abilities, and getting more of them has become his obsession. His focus on them has allowed Spider-Man to work out the pattern of the crimes and anticipate the Looter's next move.

Using other villains' signature gear helps sow confusion about who is committing Looter's crimes.

POWER RANK	ENERGY PROJECTION	STRENGTH	DURABILITY	FIGHTING SKILL	INTELLIGENCE	SPEED
	1	4	3	2	4	2

LUKE CAGE

Luke Cage is an excellent field leader, and puts his skills to good use with the New Avengers.

Framed for a crime he didn't commit, Luke Cage underwent a cruel experiment in prison that gave him superhuman strength and durability, including bulletproof skin. As Power Man, he operated a "Heroes-for-Hire" business with martial artist Iron Fist. Cage and Spider-Man frequently help each other out in their mission to clean up the streets of New York City.

Nearly indestructible, Luke Cage prefers up-close combat.

POWERFUL ALLY
Luke Cage later dropped the Power Man identity and signed on with Spider-Man as a founding member of the New Avengers. They have fought side by side against Super Villains and even an alien invasion.

VITAL STATS
REAL NAME: Luke Cage
OCCUPATION: Adventurer, vigilante
BASE: Gem Theater, New York City
HEIGHT: 6 ft 6 in (1.98 m)
WEIGHT: 425 lbs (192.78 kg)
EYES: Brown
HAIR: Black (shaved)
ORIGIN: Human mutate; gained powers in a scientific experiment
POWERS: Thanks to a serum similar to Captain America's, Luke Cage has superhuman strength, stamina, and durability. A superb athlete, he has taught himself unarmed combat techniques.

ENERGY PROJECTION	STRENGTH	DURABILITY	FIGHTING SKILL	INTELLIGENCE	SPEED
1	4	5	4	3	2

POWER RANK

LYLA

Lyla (LYrate Lifeform Approximation) is a holographic personal assistant to Miguel O'Hara, the Spider-Man of 2099, and one of the few beings that he trusts. As well as being able to access a vast range of information and communication systems, Lyla can create holographic projections that are indistinguishable from reality. This ability extends to creating illusory "clothes" for Miguel over his spider-suit, so that he can become Spider-Man at a moment's notice.

Lyla helps defeat the Scorpion by creating an illusion to make him look like Spider-Man (Peter Parker), causing him to be attacked by Spider-Slayer robots.

VITAL STATS

REAL NAME: LYrate Lifeform Approximation
OCCUPATION: Personal assistant
BASE: Nueva York, Earth-928
HEIGHT: Variable
WEIGHT: 0 lbs (0 kg)
EYES: Yellow **HAIR:** Blond
ORIGIN: Artificial intelligence; created in Earth-928 (a possible future of Earth-616) as an assistant to that world's Spider-Man, Miguel O'Hara
POWERS: Lyla's holographic projectors allow her to create illusions, while her advanced AI includes a probability matrix to predict future events.

Lyla's appearance evokes the glamor of mid-20th-century Hollywood.

SYSTEM VULNERABILITIES
As an AI, Lyla is vulnerable to cyberattack. On one occasion, a computer virus caused Lyla to attack Miguel O'Hara's girlfriend. However, Lyla later used this perceived weakness to fool the android Electro from 2099 into believing that he had broken her programming, and had persuaded her to betray Miguel in exchange for her freedom.

Although she can create holographic projections of all colors, Lyla always appears in gold.

POWER RANK

	ENERGY PROJECTION	STRENGTH	DURABILITY	FIGHTING SKILL	INTELLIGENCE	SPEED
	1	1	3	1	5	1

MADAME WEB

Cassandra Webb possessed the mutant ability to read minds. As the fortune teller Madame Web, she passed information to Spider-Man concerning his cases and also served as a mentor to Mattie Franklin, the fourth Spider-Woman. Tragedy struck when she and Mattie died at the hands of the Kravinoff family, but Madame Web managed to transfer her powers—and her title—to Julia Carpenter.

Madame Web's ties with Spider-Man made her a target of the Kravinoff family, who tried to use her to control Spidey's future.

Though blind, Madame Web could see into the past, present, and future.

TRANSFORMATIONS
In a mystic ceremony known as the Gathering of Five, Madame Web gained a more youthful appearance and enhanced mobility. However she was aged again while trying to subdue her villainous spider-powered granddaughter, Charlotte Witter.

Her spider-like chair was also a life-support system.

VITAL STATS
REAL NAME: Cassandra Webb
OCCUPATION: Clairvoyant
BASE: New York City
HEIGHT: 5 ft 6 in (1.68 m)
WEIGHT: 110 lbs (49.9 kg)
EYES: Gray
HAIR: Black
ORIGIN: Mutant
POWERS: Madame Web has great telepathic powers and can predict future events. She can appear to others in spirit form. She depends on a cybernetic web to stay alive.

ENERGY PROJECTION	STRENGTH	DURABILITY	FIGHTING SKILL	INTELLIGENCE	SPEED
1	1	1	1	4	1

POWER RANK

MAGGIA

The Maggia is a criminal consortium of influential families. Led by the Silvermane, Hammerhead, and Nefaria families, the Maggia syndicate is an enemy of Spider-Man and of the forces of law and order in New York City.

KEY MEMBERS

Silvermane: Criminal mastermind; cyborg body gives him superhuman strength, speed, and durability.

Count Nefaria: Criminal scientist; body is scientifically enhanced to give him vast strength, but makes him a vampire.

Hammerhead: Super-strong crime boss with an adamantium cranium.

AGENTS EVERYWHERE

Spider-Man has fought the Maggia's agents dozens of times, even though they often keep their true allegiance a secret. The Maggia gained its lofty criminal status by always keeping its schemes in shadow, leaving the police with no evidence to use for prosecution.

MARCY KANE

At Empire State University, Peter Parker became friends with, and occasionally dated, biophysics teaching assistant Marcy Kane. Peter kept his Super Hero identity secret from Marcy, unaware that she had one of her own—she came from beyond the stars!

An alien from the planet Contraxia, Marcy came to Earth seeking ways to save her world, whose sun was dying.

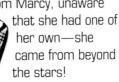

CLOSE ENCOUNTERS
Marcy Kane, whose original name was Kaina, arrived on Earth looking for a way to reignite the dying sun of her homeworld, Contraxia. Operating undercover at Empire State University, Marcy learned from brilliant scientists like Peter Parker while investigating experimental technologies.

Marcy's plain and simple wardrobe fits in with her role as a teacher.

Knowledge of extraterrestrial science helped Marcy get her university post.

VITAL STATS
REAL NAMES: Kaina
OCCUPATION: Biophysicist
BASE: Contraxia
HEIGHT: 5 ft 6 in (1.68 m)
WEIGHT: 120 lbs (54.43 kg)
EYES: White
HAIR: Brown
ORIGIN: Alien (Contraxian)
POWERS: Marcy is an alien from the planet Contraxia with an extensive knowledge of advanced extraterrestrial science. She is a trained undercover agent.

ENERGY PROJECTION	STRENGTH	DURABILITY	FIGHTING SKILL	INTELLIGENCE	SPEED
1	2	2	2	4	2

POWER RANK

MARY JANE WATSON

Peter Parker didn't know how he could ever settle down with a fun-loving, free spirit like Mary Jane Watson, but she proved to be the love of his life. MJ's feisty personality complements Peter's seriousness, and their love has persisted through the years in the face of many challenges.

In their very first meeting, Mary Jane dazzled Peter. He soon grew to love her attitude to life.

VITAL STATS
REAL NAME: Mary Jane "MJ" Watson
OCCUPATION: Actress
BASE: New York City
HEIGHT: 5 ft 8 in (1.73 m)
WEIGHT: 120 lbs (54.43 kg)
EYES: Green
HAIR: Red
ORIGIN: Human
POWERS: Mary Jane is a talented model, actress, and dancer with a fun-loving, outgoing personality—and she is good at keeping secrets!

MJ works as an actress and model.

MJ has known Spider-Man's secret identity for a long time.

PETER MEETS HIS MATCH
Peter resisted the efforts of his Aunt May to hook him up with the girl next door, but changed his mind once he met Mary Jane. The two began dating following the tragic death of Peter's girlfriend Gwen Stacy. On the night that Peter's uncle was murdered, MJ saw Peter leaving his house dressed as Spider-Man and guessed his secret, although she hid her discovery from him for a long time. Peter trusts her completely, and has saved her life many times.

POWER RANK	ENERGY PROJECTION	STRENGTH	DURABILITY	FIGHTING SKILL	INTELLIGENCE	SPEED
	1	2	2	2	2	2

MARY AND RICHARD PARKER

Raised by his Aunt May and Uncle Ben, Peter Parker never knew his real parents, CIA agents Richard and Mary Parker. They died on a mission with many believing them traitors, but in reality they saved the world several times over. Years later, Peter cleared their names, and even managed to learn a little more about them when he discovered an old safe house of theirs with his sister Teresa.

Although their work was highly important, Mary and Richard dreamed of one day leaving it behind to be a normal family.

SECRET AGENTS
Richard and Mary Parker were trained operatives working for U.S. security. They were both highly intelligent, and while no stronger than normal, physically fit adults, they were exceptionally skilled at hand-to-hand combat and with firearms.

Mary and Richard were trained by the U.S. government.

MENACE

No one knew that well-connected girl about town Lily Hollister was secretly Menace, a villain amped up on Goblin serum and wielding a variety of Goblin-related weaponry. When the truth came out, Lily gave up her baby to his father Harry Osborn and joined the Goblin Nation. She was later cured of her condition by Spider-Man, but returned to villainy under a new alias, Queen Cat.

Spider-Man fought Menace when she arrived on the scene, not realizing that Norman Osborn would soon recruit her as a powerful new member in his schemes.

VITAL STATS

REAL NAME: Lily Hollister
OCCUPATION: Vigilante, fugitive; former socialite, criminal
BASE: Gramercy Park, New York City
HEIGHT: 5 ft 6 in (1.68 m); 6 ft (1.83 m) (as Menace)
WEIGHT: 116 lbs (52.62 kg); 174 lbs (78.93 kg) (as Menace)
EYES: Brown (green as Menace)
HAIR: Blond (red as Menace)
ORIGIN: Human mutate; enhanced via the Goblin serum
POWERS: Menace uses weaponry and equipment stolen from the original Green Goblin, Norman Osborn. The Goblin serum gives her superhuman strength, stamina, speed, and agility.

The Green Goblin serum gives Lily a devilish appearance.

JOINING THE FAMILY
Menace fought Spider-Man and earned the respect of Norman Osborn, who welcomed her as a new member of the Green Goblin family. She formed an alliance with Norman against her ex-lover, Harry. Menace later had Harry Osborn's baby, but left the child with Spider-Man, fearing that she was an unfit mother. She later teamed up with the Goblin King.

Lily's appearance after taking the Goblin serum varies: sometimes she appears almost human, other times more demonic.

POWER RANK

ENERGY PROJECTION	STRENGTH	DURABILITY	FIGHTING SKILL	INTELLIGENCE	SPEED
4	4	5	3	3	3

MENDEL STROMM

Mendel Stromm's love of gadgets brought him comfort in a troubled childhood. As an adult he became Norman Osborn's business partner, using his scientific genius to build success for Oscorp, but a jealous Osborn had him jailed. After Stromm was released, he sought revenge on Osborn. Although they had a common enemy, Stromm clashed with Spider-Man several times.

Although Mendel Stromm didn't know it, his arrest was orchestrated by Norman Osborn as a result of a deal Osborn made with the demonic Mephisto.

TWISTED SCIENCE
It was Mendel Stromm who came up with the Goblin Formula, used to such tragic effect by Norman Osborn and others. In fact, Stromm had taken some of the formula himself, enabling him to evade death on several occasions. He also used his robotics knowledge to prolong his life by building artificial bodies as his own deteriorated.

Stromm took the alias of the Robot Master, and frequently used armies of robots to carry out his plans.

Stromm has cheated death many times by transferring his body and consciousness into a cyborg construction.

VITAL STATS
REAL NAME: Mendel Stromm
OCCUPATION: Scientist, inventor, Super Villain
BASE: New York City
HEIGHT: 5 ft 10 in (1.78 m)
WEIGHT: 150 lbs (68 kg)
EYES: Blue   **HAIR:** None
ORIGIN: Human mutate and cyborg; survived near-fatal injuries several times by being infused with Goblin Formula and integrated with various robot bodies
POWERS: Stromm is a genius scientist in the fields of chemistry and robotics. The Goblin Formula gives him enhanced durability, and his robot body enables him to network with various technology systems.

ENERGY PROJECTION	STRENGTH	DURABILITY	FIGHTING SKILL	INTELLIGENCE	SPEED
1	3	4	2	5	2

POWER RANK

MEPHISTO

The demon Mephisto is a being of unimaginable power. While Aunt May lay dying from a gunshot wound, Peter Parker looked to his magical allies for help. When his efforts proved fruitless, Peter made a deal with Mephisto. The demon restored Aunt May to health, but at the cost of wiping Peter's marriage to Mary Jane from history.

Mephisto is not satisfied with his underworld role, and wishes to control the lives of mortals.

VITAL STATS
REAL NAME: Mephisto
OCCUPATION: Trickster, ruler of an extra-dimensional "Hell"
BASE: Hotel Inferno, Las Vegas, Nevada
HEIGHT: 6 ft 6 in (1.98 m)
WEIGHT: 310 lbs (140.61 kg)
EYES: White
HAIR: Black
ORIGIN: Demon
POWERS: Mephisto has limitless magical powers, strength, and stamina. He is immortal, can shape-shift, and can possess the souls of those who willingly surrender them.

If he wishes, Mephisto can disguise his true form.

The limits of Mephisto's powers are unknown.

WARPING REALITY
Mephisto agreed to erase the marriage of Peter and Mary Jane, knowing that it would leave behind an echo of painful loss for Mephisto to enjoy for eternity. Mephisto's reality-warping abilities triggered a permanent change in the timeline, leaving no one with memories of Peter and Mary Jane's relationship.

POWER RANK

ENERGY PROJECTION	STRENGTH	DURABILITY	FIGHTING SKILL	INTELLIGENCE	SPEED
			2		

MIRAGE

One of the world's top specialists in the field of three-dimensional holograms, Desmond Charne decided to exploit his expertise by becoming the villainous Mirage. His costume incorporates miniature holographic projectors that can generate illusions and even turn him invisible—handy tricks when facing a foe as resourceful, agile, and strong as Spider-Man!

If Spider-Man can connect with a punch, he can knock out Mirage. The trick is finding the true target!

HOPING FOR HIS BIG BREAK
Mirage earned a bad reputation when he tried to rob the guests at Betty Brant and Ned Leeds' wedding. Spider-Man put him behind bars, and Mirage later died at the hands of an underworld vigilante. He has since returned to life and serves as a member of the Hood's criminal army.

Costume is fitted with holographic technology.

VITAL STATS
REAL NAME: Desmond Charne
OCCUPATION: Criminal, engineer, inventor
BASE: New York City
HEIGHT: 5 ft 11 in (1.8 m)
WEIGHT: 195 lbs (88.45 kg)
EYES: Blue
HAIR: Unknown
ORIGIN: Human
POWERS: Mirage projects holographs to help commit crimes with his gang. His gun fires tranquilizer darts as well as bullets.

ENERGY PROJECTION	STRENGTH	DURABILITY	FIGHTING SKILL	INTELLIGENCE	SPEED
3	2	2	2	2	2

POWER RANK

MISS ARROW

A reborn Spider-Man emerged from a cocoon after a battle with Morlun, but the discarded husk of his old self came to life as his wicked opposite. This being called itself "The Other" and later went undercover as Miss Arrow, a nurse at Midtown High School. She hid her true nature while keeping an eye on fellow faculty member Peter Parker and waiting for her time to strike.

Once she dropped her convincing human disguise, Miss Arrow could use all of her spider powers against Spider-Man.

VITAL STATS
REAL NAME: The Other
OCCUPATION: Mystical predator
BASE: Mobile
HEIGHT: 5 ft 4 in (1.63 m)
WEIGHT: 105 lbs (47.63 kg)
EYES: Hazel (as Miss Arrow)
HAIR: Blond (as Miss Arrow)
ORIGIN: Totemic deity
POWERS: Miss Arrow could control and command the spiders that made up her body. She could also transform into a swarm of spiders. Spider-stingers on her wrists could inject venom.

Body could break into many smaller spiders.

Miss Arrow's name came from the Latin Ero, a genus of so-called pirate spiders that eat other spiders.

A MONSTER IN DISGUISE
Miss Arrow developed an attraction to Flash Thompson, who was working at Midtown High School as a sports coach. When Flash refused to become her new host, Miss Arrow burst into thousands of spiders and attacked him. Spider-Man arrived just in time to end her threat.

POWER RANK	ENERGY PROJECTION	STRENGTH	DURABILITY	FIGHTING SKILL	INTELLIGENCE	SPEED
	2	4	3	4	4	3

Though a recent arrival in New York's underworld, Mister Negative has quickly become one of its most powerful players.

MISTER NEGATIVE

Mister Negative is the dark side of kindly Martin Li, who operates a soup kitchen in New York City's Chinatown. A dose of experimental chemicals caused Li's "Mister Negative" personality to emerge, and he set out to become the city's biggest crime boss. Mister Negative's incredible healing powers also resulted in the creation of Anti-Venom.

When he powers up, Mister Negative appears as a reverse black-and-white image.

DECEPTIVELY DANGEROUS
Mister Negative tried to corrupt Peter Parker's Aunt May when she volunteered to help at his soup kitchen. He is accompanied by his Inner Demons, a group of heavily armed bodyguards with powerful healing abilities, who wear demon masks.

Mister Negative has a corrupting touch that can turn good people bad and get them to do his bidding.

VITAL STATS
REAL NAME: Unknown
OCCUPATION: Crime lord
BASE: Shanghai, China
HEIGHT: 5 ft 11 in (1.8 m)
WEIGHT: 180 lbs (81.65 kg)
EYES: Brown (white as Mister Negative)
HAIR: Black (white as Mister Negative)
ORIGIN: Human mutated by Darkforce and Lightforce
POWERS: Martin Li has powers associated with the Darkforce Dimension, such as shape-shifting, and a healing or corrupting touch. As well as superhuman strength, he has the ability to control others.

ENERGY PROJECTION	STRENGTH	DURABILITY	FIGHTING SKILL	INTELLIGENCE	SPEED	POWER RANK
4	5	4	4	3	3	

MOLTEN MAN

An industrial accident left scientist Mark Raxton coated from head to toe in a liquid metal alloy. He pursued a criminal career as the Molten Man, but his condition worsened until his metal skin grew so hot it threatened to burn him alive. Mark's stepsister, Liz Allan, helped him, causing him to rediscover the value of human kindness. Eventually, due to her position as head of Alchemax, Liz managed to discover a cure for Mark's condition.

The incredibly painful transformation into a being of burning metal made Mark Raxton a tragic figure.

VITAL STATS
REAL NAME: Mark Raxton
OCCUPATION: Scientist
BASE: Alchemax Tower, New York City
HEIGHT: 6 ft 5 in (1.96 m)
WEIGHT: 255 lbs (115.67 kg)
EYES: Hazel
HAIR: Blond
ORIGIN: Human mutate; his body absorbed an experimental molten alloy that he tried to steal from fellow scientist Spencer Smythe
POWERS: Molten Man can slip from any grasp and has superhuman strength. He can make his body so hot that it can melt most materials. His slightest touch can cause severe burns.

HELPING WHERE HE CAN
The Molten Man occasionally lends a hand to Spider-Man. However, he has difficulty controlling his emotions, and if he feels that his family members are in danger the Molten Man can become a boiling cauldron of white-hot rage.

The Molten Man throws punches that can melt iron.

POWER RANK

ENERGY PROJECTION	STRENGTH	DURABILITY	FIGHTING SKILL	INTELLIGENCE	SPEED
2	5	5	3	3	2

MOON KNIGHT

Marc Spector was a soldier-for-hire, until an assignment in Egypt left him near death. Revived by the Egyptian God of Vengeance Khonshu, Marc became Moon Knight. His personal fortune funds his crime-fighting, and he carries an array of throwing blades and other specialty weapons. Moon Knight is one of Spider-Man's nocturnal allies.

His wealth allows Moon Knight to employ a large number of crime-fighting devices, including motorcycles and helicopters.

On his costume, Moon Knight bears the crescent moon symbol of Khonshu.

MULTIPLE PERSONALITIES
Unlike Spider-Man, Moon Knight maintains more than one secret identity. As wealthy financier Steven Grant he mingles with high society, while he gets a street-level view of the action by posing as taxi driver Jake Lockley.

Moon Knight carries a wide variety of weapons, including pistols.

VITAL STATS
REAL NAME: Marc Spector
OCCUPATION: Adventurer, vigilante, millionaire entrepreneur
BASE: New York City
HEIGHT: 6 ft 2 in (1.88 m)
WEIGHT: 225 lbs (102.06 kg)
EYES: Brown
HAIR: Brown
ORIGIN: Human granted moon-based powers by an idol of the Egyptian Moon God, Khonshu
POWERS: Moon Knight wields various weapons given to him by Khonshu. He has great strength and durability but his powers wax and wane with the phases of the moon.

ENERGY PROJECTION	STRENGTH	DURABILITY	FIGHTING SKILL	INTELLIGENCE	SPEED
1	3	3	3	2	2

POWER RANK

MORBIUS

Morbius has the fangs, the bloodlust, and the weakness to sunlight of a true vampire, but his powers don't have a supernatural origin. Transformed by an experimental blood serum, Dr. Michael Morbius contracted "pseudo-vampirism" to become Morbius, the Living Vampire! His greatest wish is to be rid of his condition forever.

When his heroic instincts win out, Morbius works to help the Super Hero community in their fight against evil forces.

VITAL STATS

REAL NAME: Michael Morbius
OCCUPATION: Nobel Prize winning biochemist, criminal scientist
BASE: Mobile
HEIGHT: 5 ft 10 in (1.78 m)
WEIGHT: 170 lbs (77.11 kg)
EYES: Red
HAIR: Black
ORIGIN: Human mutate; exposed to an experimental serum
POWERS: Morbius has enhanced strength, speed, and senses, powers of hypnosis and gliding, and sharp fangs and claws. He is a genius-level scientist.

HUNTING FOR A CURE
Morbius the Living Vampire secretly worked with Horizon Labs to create a cure for New York's spider-virus. He hoped this role might help him to find his own salvation, but instead he was met with hostility by government investigators when his identity was revealed.

Morbius does not have the usual vulnerabilities of a vampire, although he is more sensitive to sunlight than an ordinary human.

Spider-Man tries to help Morbius, but the Living Vampire's killer instinct is strong.

	ENERGY PROJECTION	STRENGTH	DURABILITY	FIGHTING SKILL	INTELLIGENCE	SPEED
POWER RANK	1	4	4	2	5	3

MORLUN

Morlun has walked the Earth for centuries, feeding on the life-forces of lesser beings while seeking out the pure energy of "totems," the human avatars of primal animal spirits. Believing Spider-Man to be the bearer of the spider-totem, Morlun tracked him relentlessly, hoping to consume the spider's essence and prolong his own life.

Morlun came close to ending Spider-Man's life, but the web-swinger battled back from the brink of death to defeat his tormentor.

Morlun's old-fashioned attire indicates his age.

PRIMAL PREDATOR
Spider-Man and the mysterious Ezekiel teamed up to defeat Morlun, seemingly wiping him from existence. But Morlun has returned from the dead several times since then, drawing on his connection to the spiritual energy of living beings to fuel his resurrections.

Morlun can seemingly appear and disappear at will.

VITAL STATS
REAL NAME: Morlun
OCCUPATION: Hunter of super-powered beings
BASE: Sims Tower, New York City
HEIGHT: 6 ft 2 in (1.88 m)
WEIGHT: 175 lbs (79.38 kg)
EYES: Red
HAIR: Black
ORIGIN: Psychic vampire
POWERS: Morlun absorbs the life-forces of other beings. His strength varies depending on how recently he has fed.

ENERGY PROJECTION	STRENGTH	DURABILITY	FIGHTING SKILL	INTELLIGENCE	SPEED
1	4	3	4	3	3

POWER RANK

MS. MARVEL

Kamala Khan is an ordinary teenager from Jersey City when she is transformed by the Terrigen Mist. It awakens her latent Inhuman DNA, and she discovers that she now has the power to change the shape and size of her body. A big fan of Super Heroes, Kamala is excited to join their ranks, eventually achieving her dream of becoming an Avenger. Later, she forms a team with Spider-Man (Miles Morales) and other young heroes: the Champions.

Although a longtime super-fan of Carol Danvers, the original Ms. Marvel, Kamala realized that she would have to tread her own path and stamp her own identity on the Ms. Marvel alias.

VITAL STATS
REAL NAME: Kamala Khan
OCCUPATION: Super Hero
BASE: Jersey City
HEIGHT: 5 ft 4 in (1.63 m) (variable)
WEIGHT: 125 lbs (57 kg) (variable)
EYES: Brown
HAIR: Brown
ORIGIN: Inhuman; underwent Terrigenesis after detonation of a Terrigen Bomb, triggering latent stretching powers
POWERS: Ms. Marvel has the ability to change her shape and size dramatically, including being able to imitate other people or objects. She has an enhanced healing factor.

Kamala's friend Bruno created her suit from biokinetic polymer so that it would stretch with her body as she used her powers.

Kamala created her own spin on Carol Danvers' Ms. Marvel costume, keeping the iconic lightning bolt on the front.

STRETCHING TIME
Ms. Marvel's ability to stretch or compress her body is even more incredible than it first appears. When she uses her powers, she is in fact either taking or giving mass at a molecular level from past and future versions of herself—almost like traveling in time.

POWER RANK

ENERGY PROJECTION	STRENGTH	DURABILITY	FIGHTING SKILL	INTELLIGENCE	SPEED
1	4	4	1	2	3

MYSTERIO

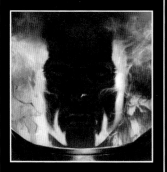

Hollywood stuntman and special-effects whiz Quentin Beck learned that crime could pay after he quit his job and became the villain Mysterio. Whenever Spider-Man fights Mysterio, he has a tough time figuring out what's real and what's an illusion!

Though he tries to make it appear as if he has mystical powers, Mysterio relies on mind control and stagecraft tricks.

Helmet protects from smoke used to confuse opponents.

UNFINISHED BUSINESS
Mysterio originally wished to take Spider-Man's place as a Super Hero, until Spidey put a stop to his scheming. Mysterio later died, but seemingly returned from the afterlife to continue to vex Spider-Man. He worked for Sasha Kravinoff as part of a plot to bring her husband, Kraven the Hunter, back to the land of the living so that he could get revenge on Spider-Man.

Mysterio can conceal weapons beneath his cloak.

VITAL STATS
REAL NAME: Quentin Beck
OCCUPATION: Criminal mastermind; former Hollywood special-effects designer and stuntman
BASE: Ravencroft institute
HEIGHT: 5 ft 11 in (1.8 m)
WEIGHT: 175 lbs (79.38 kg)
EYES: Blue
HAIR: Black
ORIGIN: Human
POWERS: Mysterio was once a leading movie special-effects designer, and uses his ability to create illusions in order to commit crimes and confuse Spider-Man. He is also a skilled hypnotist.

ENERGY PROJECTION	STRENGTH	DURABILITY	FIGHTING SKILL	INTELLIGENCE	SPEED
4	3		3	3	2

POWER RANK

NED LEEDS

Peter Parker and Ned worked together at *The Daily Bugle*, where Ned met and married administrative assistant Betty Brant. Then Roderick Kingsley, the evil Hobgoblin, brainwashed Ned into acting as a decoy for his own activities. Criminals murdered Ned thinking he was the Hobgoblin, but the Goblin serum in his blood enabled him to be resurrected a few days later.

In a rare moment of happiness, Ned married Betty Brant—only to have the villain Mirage interrupt the ceremony.

VITAL STATS

REAL NAME: Edward "Ned" Leeds
OCCUPATION: Reporter
BASE: Formerly Daily Bugle Building, New York City
HEIGHT: 5 ft 11 in (1.8 m)
WEIGHT: 205 lbs (92.99 kg)
EYES: Blue
HAIR: Blond
ORIGIN: Human
POWERS: Ned was an experienced newspaper reporter. Under the influence of Roderick Kingsley he briefly used the Hobgoblin's weapons and equipment.

FAKE NEWS

A rival of Peter Parker for the affections of Betty Brant, Ned won Betty's heart but later emerged as the primary suspect for the crimes committed by the Hobgoblin. After Ned's death Peter proved his innocence, though many people still believed that Ned had lived a villainous double life.

Ned's reunion with his wife after his apparent death came when he provided information for a story she was investigating.

POWER RANK

ENERGY PROJECTION	STRENGTH	DURABILITY	FIGHTING SKILL	INTELLIGENCE	SPEED
1	2	2	2	2	2

NICK FURY JR.

U.S. Army Ranger Marcus Johnson discovers that his real father is elite secret agent Nick Fury, and that he carries the powers of the Infinity Formula in his blood. Following his father into the world of espionage and joining S.H.I.E.L.D., Marcus also finds out that his true name is Nick Fury, Jr. He is joined in his new career by former army colleague Phil Coulson.

Fury is given a set of Falcon's wings by Nighthawk so that he can assist him in finding the Infinity Stones.

Like his father, Nick Fury Jr. is missing his left eye and covers the area with an eyepatch.

FINDING HIS WAY
After S.H.I.E.L.D. is dissolved, Fury falls into a life of solo espionage, driven by a desire to keep protecting the world. He is able to get backup and materiel for his chosen missions by using the inside knowledge he has on those in power as leverage, and what he describes as a "creative interpretation" of the Patriot Act..

His battlesuit is more than it appears, featuring a stealth mode and the ability to inject chemicals for a temporary physical boost.

VITAL STATS
REAL NAME: Nicholas J. Fury Jr.
OCCUPATION: Spy
BASE: Mobile
HEIGHT: 6 ft 3 in (1.91 m)
WEIGHT: 225 lbs (102 kg)
EYES: Brown
HAIR: Black
ORIGIN: Human mutate; secret child of Nick Fury Sr. who discovers his true parentage in adulthood and follows his father's footsteps into S.H.I.E.L.D.
POWERS: Inheritance of the Infinity Formula gives Fury decelerated aging, and physical condition at or slightly beyond peak human levels.

ENERGY PROJECTION	STRENGTH	DURABILITY	FIGHTING SKILL	INTELLIGENCE	SPEED	POWER RANK
1	3	3	6	3	2	

NIGHTMARE

When people fall asleep and start to dream, that's when Nightmare is at his most dangerous! He prowls an otherworldly dimension on his black steed Dreamstalker, gaining power from sleepers' nightmares and pushing dreamers further into fear and madness. Can Spider-Man defeat this nocturnal reign of terror?

In the dream realm, Nightmare has almost limitless powers. Spider-Man must face his worst fears to beat the demon.

VITAL STATS

REAL NAME: Nightmare
OCCUPATION: Ruler of the Nightmare World, deity
BASE: Nightmare World, Dream Dimension
HEIGHT: Variable
WEIGHT: Variable
EYES: Green
HAIR: Black
ORIGIN: Extradimensional demonic entity
POWERS: Nightmare is a demon of great mystical power who usually targets victims when they are asleep. He can teleport.

Nightmare is much less powerful outside his home realm.

BAD DREAMS
Nightmare is the arch-enemy of the sorcerer Doctor Strange, but Spider-Man has also been pulled into the fight. During one of Spider-Man's early adventures, Nightmare tormented him with his most feared visions, including the exposure of his secret identity.

Although a demon, Nightmare has been killed before by the Asgardian Loki.

POWER RANK

ENERGY PROJECTION	STRENGTH	DURABILITY	FIGHTING SKILL	INTELLIGENCE	SPEED
			2	2	

NORMAN OSBORN

Power-mad Norman Osborn committed more evil deeds in his own name than he ever did as the Green Goblin! With the global resources of Oscorp Industries at his disposal, Norman went underground after the Green Goblin's "death" to launch plots against Spider-Man, including the creation of Peter Parker clones.

Norman Osborn took visual inspiration from Iron Man and Captain America to create his Iron Patriot armor.

Osborn is extremely intelligent and strong-willed.

NEW HIGHS, NEW LOWS

Norman Osborn achieved success as leader of the Thunderbolts, a government-sanctioned team of reformed villains. This allowed him to become director of S.H.I.E.L.D. successor H.A.M.M.E.R. and founder of a new team, the Dark Avengers, while wearing his own suit of battle armor as the Iron Patriot. However, in time, Osborn's power-mad Green Goblin persona once again possessed him and he was removed from office in disgrace.

In his non-Goblin form, Norman often wears a smart suit befitting a top businessman.

VITAL STATS

REAL NAME: Norman Virgil Osborn

OCCUPATION: Professional criminal mastermind

BASE: Mobile

HEIGHT: 5 ft 11 in (1.8 m)

WEIGHT: 185 lbs (83.91 kg)

EYES: Green **HAIR** Auburn

ORIGIN: Human mutate; accidentally exposed to a chemical formula that increases strength and intelligence, but caused mental instability

POWERS: The Goblin serum gives Osborn superhuman physical abilities.

ENERGY PROJECTION	STRENGTH	DURABILITY	FIGHTING SKILL	INTELLIGENCE	SPEED
3	4	4	3	4	3

POWER RANK

NORMIE OSBORN

Normie Osborn was unlikely to have a peaceful childhood. As well as being a juicy target for kidnappers thanks to his family wealth and connections, Normie was also at risk from any family members who took Goblin Formula, with its corresponding effect on their sanity. Although at first blaming Spider-Man for his family's woes, Normie started to realize that much of their trouble was self-inflicted.

Peter Parker is delighted to be named Normie's godson soon after he is born, but as the boy grows he has a conflicted relationship with Spider-Man.

VITAL STATS
REAL NAME: Norman Harold Osborn
OCCUPATION: Student
BASE: New York City
HEIGHT: 3 ft 9 in (1.14 m)
WEIGHT: 45 lbs (20.41 kg)
EYES: Blue
HAIR: Brown
ORIGIN: Human; son of Harry Osborn and Liz Allan; grandson of Norman Osborn, the Green Goblin
POWERS: None, although he has had powers when bonded to the Carnage symbiote.

Normie is still growing, so it is not yet known how much his father's use of the Goblin Formula might have affected his DNA.

GOBLIN CHILDE
Normie was bonded with the Carnage symbiote by his grandfather Norman, at the time the Red Goblin. Normie became incredibly powerful as the so-called Goblin Childe, but struggled to control the symbiote as he was so young. Later, Normie was cured, but a trace of the symbiote remained in his body.

While bonded with the Carnage symbiote, Normie's powers included super-strength and agility as well as wall-crawling.

	ENERGY PROJECTION	STRENGTH	DURABILITY	FIGHTING SKILL	INTELLIGENCE	SPEED
POWER RANK	1	1	1	1	2	1

OVERDRIVE

He claims to be Spider-Man's biggest fan, but Overdrive usually works against the wall-crawler when he's hired by crime bosses such as Mr. Negative. His ability to transform any motor vehicle comes in handy when Overdrive needs to flee the scene of his latest crime, but Spider-Man usually shows up to apply the brakes.

If Spider-Man can get Overdrive out of the driver's seat, he can usually outfight him and put the villain down for the count.

Overdrive instinctually knows how to drive his transformed vehicles.

DRIVER IN DEMAND
Overdrive recently signed up as one of the Sinister Six, modifying the gigantic Big Wheel to serve as the team's getaway vehicle. When Spider-Man disrupted the Big Wheel's gyroscopic balance unit, Overdrive's ride toppled uselessly onto its side.

Upgrades can improve Overdrive's speed, armor, or weapons.

VITAL STATS
REAL NAME: James Beverly
OCCUPATION: Driver; former henchmen, criminal
BASE: New York City
HEIGHT: 5 ft 9 in (1.75 m)
WEIGHT: 165 lbs (78.84 kg)
EYES: Brown
HAIR: Black
ORIGIN: Human granted power by the Power Broker
POWERS: Overdrive disperses nanites, which greatly enhance the performance of any ground vehicle while he is at the wheel. He is a skilled race-car driver and mechanic.

ENERGY PROJECTION	STRENGTH	DURABILITY	FIGHTING SKILL	INTELLIGENCE	SPEED
2	2	3	3	2	2

POWER RANK

PALADIN

Paladin is quick to sing his own praises, but this mercenary has the skills to justify his high fee. His cases have sometimes brought him into partnership with Spider-Man, and Paladin has also worked as one of Silver Sable's Outlaws. Becoming romantically involved with private detective Misty Knight, Paladin helped her carry out a deep cover "villains-for-hire" operation to bring down the Purple Man and several other wanted criminals.

Paladin is primarily a solo operator, but he knows when he's outmatched and is willing to be a team player as long as the money is good.

VITAL STATS

REAL NAME: Unknown
OCCUPATION: Mercenary, private investigator
BASE: Mobile
HEIGHT: 6 ft 2 in (1.88 m)
WEIGHT: 225 lbs (102.06 kg)
EYES: Brown
HAIR: Brown
ORIGIN: Human
POWERS: Paladin wears a padded, bulletproof costume, carries a high-tech stun gun, and is a gifted combatant and investigator. He can also sense opponents before they attack.

Paladin's goggles have infrared capabilities.

An armored suit and plenty of weaponry keep Paladin ready for action.

READY TO ASSIST
Spider-Man knows Paladin is reliable as long as he gets paid. The two worked together to uncover a conspiracy that threatened to undermine Silver Sable's home nation of Symkaria. Paladin later joined the Thunderbolts, a team of reformed villains.

POWER RANK	ENERGY PROJECTION	STRENGTH	DURABILITY	FIGHTING SKILL	INTELLIGENCE	SPEED
	4	4	3	4	3	3

KEY MEMBERS

1. **Peter Parker:** After he regains control of his body, Peter is forced to balance life as a CEO with his activities as Spider-Man.

2. **Anna Maria Marconi:** Anna Maria is involved in Parker Industries from its foundation, becoming one of its key employees and sharpest brains.

3. **Sajani Jaffrey:** Incredibly intelligent, Sajani's ruthless attitude can nevertheless make her hard to work with.

4. **Living Brain:** Previously engineered for evil, the robot Living Brain has been upgraded, making it a valuable addition to Parker Industries.

5. **Clayton Cole:** Also known as the villain Clash, Clayton is given a job by Peter Parker to help him try and go straight.

Parker Industries is a corporation that monetizes advanced technology, and is the brainchild of Otto Octavius when he is in possession of Peter Parker's body as the Superior Spider-Man. When Peter takes over his body again, he keeps the company going despite never having seen himself as a businessman. He tries to use Parker Industries' huge resources to make the world a better place, even planning to build a facility for rehabilitating Super Villains.

Using the profits from Parker Industries, Peter Parker creates the Uncle Ben Foundation, a charity seeking to improve quality of life for the less fortunate.

PENI PARKER

After Peni Parker's father dies operating the SP//dr suit she is taken in by her Aunt May and Uncle Ben. Although she is still a child, due to her genetics she is the only person who can take over as the SP//dr, so she becomes a protector of her reality. Despite losing her Aunt May in tragic circumstances, Peni steps up to become part of the multiversal Spider-Army.

The SP//dr suit can only be operated by someone who has been bitten by the radioactive spider that forms part of its CPU.

VITAL STATS

REAL NAME: Peni Parker
OCCUPATION: Super Hero, student
BASE: New York City, Earth-14512
HEIGHT: 4 ft 11 in (1.5 m)
WEIGHT: 105 lbs (48 kg)
EYES: Brown
HAIR: Black
ORIGIN: Human mutate; inherited the capability to pilot the SP//dr suit from her father and allowed herself to be bitten by the radioactive spider linking her to the suit
POWERS: When wearing the SP//dr suit, Peni has enhanced strength, speed, and durability. She can wall-crawl and fire web projectiles from an arm-mounted weapons array.

The spider that links Peni to the SP//dr suit is with her at all times, and she has a mental link to it

Peni is highly intelligent, and helps her aunt and uncle, technicians at Oscorp, upgrade the SP//dr suit.

SUITING UP
Developed by Oscorp, the SP//dr suit is a symbiotic mech that gives its pilot various powers, including wall-crawling and firing web-fluid missiles. Peni also likes using the suit's systems to play her favorite music to help her focus in battle. However, too much power usage can drain the suit and render it immobile.

POWER RANK	ENERGY PROJECTION	STRENGTH	DURABILITY	FIGHTING SKILL	INTELLIGENCE	SPEED
	2	2	2	3	3	2

PROWLER

Hobie Brown had an inventive mind but no money to get his ideas off the ground. After Spider-Man foiled his attempt to use his gadgets in a life of crime as the Prowler, Hobie instead chose a more noble path. When Hobie adopted the new alias of the armored Hornet, Aaron Davis—who had been the Prowler on Earth-1610—took up his old identity again on Earth-616.

Spidey interrupted the Prowler's earliest crimes, leading to a new destiny for the would-be cat burglar.

The Prowler's cape helps him blend into the shadows.

RESERVE HERO
Inspired by Spider-Man's willingness to give him a second chance, the Prowler pledged himself to heroism. He later teamed up with other friends of Spider-Man as a member of the Outlaws. Prowler also occasionally helps Spidey develop new gadgets.

Talons assist in climbing walls and can also be used as weapons.

VITAL STATS
REAL NAME: Hobie Brown
OCCUPATION: Inventor; former adventurer
BASE: Mobile
HEIGHT: 5 ft 11 in (1.8 m)
WEIGHT: 180 lbs (81.65 kg)
EYES: Brown **HAIR:** Black
ORIGIN: Human
POWERS: The Prowler's costume incorporates dart-shooters and gas canisters. He is a skilled martial artist, and is a genius at inventing personal weaponry and hand-held gadgets.

ENERGY PROJECTION	STRENGTH	DURABILITY	FIGHTING SKILL	INTELLIGENCE	SPEED
3	2	2	3	4	2

POWER RANK

PUMA

Thomas Fireheart is the Puma, ancestral champion of the Native American Kisani tribe. He possesses the ability to assume the form of a human-puma hybrid. He is also the CEO of Fireheart Enterprises, and briefly became owner of *The Daily Bugle* so that he could improve public opinion of Spider-Man. He uses his experience to mentor Portal, another Kisani hero. Puma is one of the animal totems captured by Kraven for use in his Great Hunt.

Wearing his Iron Spider armor, Spider-Man teamed up with Puma and Black Cat to defeat the dinosaur villain Stegron.

VITAL STATS

REAL NAME: Thomas Fireheart
OCCUPATION: CEO of Fireheart Enterprises, occasional mercenary and assassin
BASE: Mobile
HEIGHT: 6 ft 2 in (1.88 m)
WEIGHT: 240 lbs (108.86 kg)
EYES: Green
HAIR: Black
ORIGIN: Human mutate; Fireheart is the product of many generations of mystic rituals and selective breeding
POWERS: Fireheart can transform into a werecat Puma, increasing in size and gaining enhanced senses of sight, smell, and hearing. He is highly trained in hand-to-hand combat techniques.

Sharp feline senses, especially smell, help the Puma sense danger.

SPIDER ALLY
Although they originally met as adversaries, Puma and Spider-Man are now close allies. Both heroes have served on the same team, the Outlaws, working alongside reformed villains at the request of international mercenary Silver Sable.

Extremely wealthy, the Puma can afford advanced electronic gear.

POWER RANK	ENERGY PROJECTION	STRENGTH	DURABILITY	FIGHTING SKILL	INTELLIGENCE	SPEED
	1	4	4	6	3	3

QUEEN

Reborn as the titanic Spider Queen, Adriana briefly ruled over the people of New York City.

Hoping to recreate more World War II super-soldiers like Captain America, the U.S. military experimented on Adriana Soria, transforming her into a humanoid spider. She became the Queen of all spiders, and pursued Spider-Man as her ideal mate. She believed that her power over the "insect gene" in Peter would enable her to make him do her will. Thwarted, the Queen later attempted to take over Manhattan.

The Super-Soldier serum has slowed the Queen's aging.

DEFEATING THE QUEEN
Back during World War II, Adriana briefly dated Steve Rogers, better known as Captain America. However, Cap has fought at Spider-Man's side whenever the Queen has threatened New York City. And when the Queen later mutated Cap into a "Spider-King," Spidey was on hand to help restore Cap's humanity.

Many of New York's villains bowed down to the Queen.

VITAL STATS
REAL NAME: Adriana Soria
OCCUPATION: Former U.S. Army soldier
BASE: New York City
HEIGHT: 5 ft 10 in (1.78 m)
WEIGHT: 125 lbs (56.7 kg)
EYES: Brown
HAIR: Black
ORIGIN: Mutant, spider-totem; Adriana's latent powers were activated by exposure to radiation
POWERS: Adriana can control anyone possessing the "insect gene." The Super-Soldier program has given her superhuman abilities. She also possesses a destructive sonic scream.

ENERGY PROJECTION	STRENGTH	DURABILITY	FIGHTING SKILL	INTELLIGENCE	SPEED
5	4	2	4	4	2

POWER RANK

RANDY ROBERTSON

Son of *The Daily Bugle*'s Robbie Robertson, Randy Robertson attended Empire State University along with Peter Parker. Known for his student activism and his courage in speaking up for the less fortunate, Randy pursued a career in social work. He and Peter were once roommates, and Randy is still a close friend.

Randy is often caught up in Spider-Man's adventures, but he doesn't know that Spidey is his friend Peter.

VITAL STATS

REAL NAME: Randolph "Randy" Robertson
OCCUPATION: Social worker; former student
BASE: New York City
HEIGHT: 6 ft (1.83 m)
WEIGHT: 185 lbs (83.91 kg)
EYES: Brown
HAIR Black
ORIGIN: Human
POWERS: Randy has no super-powers, but is an excellent journalist and is committed to whatever good cause he champions.

MAKING HIS WAY
In addition to social work, Randy has dabbled in acting and as a videographer for *The Daily Bugle*. During an outbreak of spider-powers across New York City caused by the Queen, Randy temporarily gained super-strength and the ability to stick to walls—until Spider-Man put an end to the Queen's bizarre and frightening reign.

Randy is a quick thinker with a stubborn streak.

Randy fell in love with Janice Lincoln (Beetle), the daughter of Tombstone, his father Robbie Robertson's nemesis.

POWER RANK	ENERGY PROJECTION	STRENGTH	DURABILITY	FIGHTING SKILL	INTELLIGENCE	SPEED
	1	2	2	2	2	2

RED GOBLIN

Red Goblin's Carnage-bombs each have a piece of the Carnage symbiote inside them—Red Goblin can speak through them and deliver painful, fanged bites as well as cause explosions.

Norman Osborn uses the Carnage symbiote to override the nanites that Spider-Man implanted to stop him becoming the Green Goblin again. As the symbiote combines with Osborn's Green Goblin powers, the ultimate hybrid is created— the Red Goblin. Fearsomely strong, the Red Goblin has almost no weaknesses, but Spider-Man uses Osborn's arrogance against him, tricking him into shedding Carnage and fighting alone.

NO LIMITS
Norman Osborn is willing to give up his sanity to regain his powers, and that is exactly what the Carnage symbiote does. After a battle with Spider-Man in which he strikes at not only the wall-crawler's friends and family but also his own, Osborn's mind is broken and he believes himself to be Cletus Kasady, the original Carnage host.

Red Goblin has no need of the armor that Green Goblin wears, having instead a powerful healing factor.

Unlike some symbiotes, Red Goblin is not vulnerable to fire or loud noises, but he can be hurt by Anti-Venom.

VITAL STATS
REAL NAME: Norman Osborn
OCCUPATION: Super Villain
BASE: New York City
HEIGHT: 5 ft 11 in (1.80 m)
WEIGHT: 185 lbs (84 kg)
EYES: Yellow
HAIR: None
ORIGIN: Human mutate bonded with alien symbiote
POWERS: Bonded with the Carnage symbiote, Osborn regains his Green Goblin powers—super-strength, speed, stamina, durability, agility, and reflexes—and adds a few more, including wall-crawling, web-shooting, shape-shifting, and an enhanced healing factor.

ENERGY PROJECTION	STRENGTH	DURABILITY	FIGHTING SKILL	INTELLIGENCE	SPEED
3	5	5	3	4	3

POWER RANK

REED RICHARDS

Genius Reed Richards designed the spacecraft for the mission that gave him and his companions super-powers, and under the name Mister Fantastic he founded the Fantastic Four. Reed encourages Spider-Man's scientific curiosity as a mentor. Married to Sue Storm (Invisible Woman), Reed is also the father of Franklin and Valeria Richards.

Reed Richards' knowledge has earned him a place among an elite group—whose members also include Iron Man and Doctor Strange—who work to shape Earth's future.

VITAL STATS

REAL NAME:
Reed Richards
OCCUPATION:
Scientist, adventurer;
former cosmic being
BASE: 4 Yancy Street,
New York City
HEIGHT: 6 ft 1 in (1.85 m)
(variable)
WEIGHT: 180 lbs (81.65 kg)
EYES: Brown
HAIR: Brown (white at temples)
ORIGIN: Human mutate; exposed
to cosmic radiation
POWERS: Reed can stretch
his body into any shape. However
his most amazing ability is his
natural scientific genius.

Reed can use his elasticity to absorb the force of a projectile and hurl it back at an opponent.

BOUNDLESS KNOWLEDGE
Reed Richards is an expert in almost every field. He sees Peter Parker as a worthy student of the sciences and encourages him in his studies. He is one of the few who knows Peter's secret identity as Spider-Man.

As well as stretching, Reed can compress his body down to small sizes.

POWER RANK	ENERGY PROJECTION	STRENGTH	DURABILITY	FIGHTING SKILL	INTELLIGENCE	SPEED
	1	2	5	3		2

Rio deploys her formidable mother Gloria when she needs to improve her son's behavior.

RIO MORALES

Rio Morales is the fiercely devoted mom of Miles Morales, aka Spider-Man. When the family are recreated on Earth-616, unlike in her previous reality she is unaware that her son is a Super Hero. When she finds out, she is hurt that both Miles and her husband Jeff have been keeping this secret from her. She learns to live with the fact that Miles is Spider-Man, but she never stops feeling protective of him.

As a nurse, Rio knows just how dangerous the streets of Brooklyn can be.

PAST LIFE
In her original reality of Earth-1610, Rio was tragically killed in the crossfire of a police battle with the villain Venom. Her son was devastated, but the family were miraculously reunited when the multiverse was largely remade by Molecule Man in the fallout of Secret Wars. Rio was restored to life on Earth-616.

Rio is originally from Puerto Rico

VITAL STATS
REAL NAME: Rio Morales
OCCUPATION: Nurse
BASE: Brooklyn, New York City
HEIGHT: 5 ft 10 in (1.78 m)
WEIGHT: 135 lbs (61 kg)
EYES: Brown
HAIR: Brown
ORIGIN: Human; originally from Earth-1610
POWERS: Rio has no super-powers, but she is medically trained and is a skilled nurse.

ENERGY PROJECTION	STRENGTH	DURABILITY	FIGHTING SKILL	INTELLIGENCE	SPEED	POWER RANK
1	1	1	1	2	1	

RHINO

If the Rhino's headed toward you, get out of the way! Thug Aleksei Sytsevich became permanently bonded to a tough exoskeleton and went into business as an unstoppable enforcer. Not big in the brains department, Rhino sells his services to smarter villains who tell him what to do.

The Rhino knows he's not the smartest villain in town, and gets angry at the thought that people are laughing at him behind his back.

VITAL STATS

REAL NAME: Aleksei Mikhailovich Sytsevich
OCCUPATION: Professional criminal
BASE: Formerly Transamerica Pyramid, San Francisco
HEIGHT: 6 ft 5 in (1.96 m)
WEIGHT: 710 lbs (322.05 kg)
EYES: Brown **HAIR:** Brown
ORIGIN: Human mutate; body was transformed by gamma radiation
POWERS: Gamma radiation gives Rhino superhuman strength, speed, and durability. His powers are greatly enhanced by an armored polymer exoskeleton that has the appearance of Rhino skin.

Rhino's armor boosts his already impressive strength and durability.

A FAMILIAR FOE
Rhino has suffered a string of defeats trying to beat Spider-Man, but remains committed to the only life he has ever known. An experiment once gave Rhino a genius-level intellect, but he lost it just as suddenly.

Spider-Man's best strategy is to stay out of the Rhino's reach.

POWER RANK

ENERGY PROJECTION	STRENGTH	DURABILITY	FIGHTING SKILL	INTELLIGENCE	SPEED
1	6	5	3	2	3

ROBBIE ROBERTSON

One of the most respected staffers on *The Daily Bugle*, Joe "Robbie" Robertson helped Peter when he joined the staff of the newspaper as a photographer. For many years Robbie was a calm contrast to fiery editor-in-chief J. Jonah Jameson. He later became the paper's publisher.

Robbie was brave enough to stand up to J. Jonah Jameson's volcanic rages, and sometimes even made him see reason!

Robbie has great respect for Peter Parker's skills as a journalist.

PAST SECRETS
For years Robbie was haunted by his failure to speak out against the hitman Tombstone. Spider-Man eventually helped him bring the killer to justice, and Robbie is proud to call Spidey his friend. Under Robbie's leadership, *The Daily Bugle* took a much more positive view of Spider-Man's heroics.

The *Bugle*'s reporters know they'll be treated fairly under Robbie's leadership.

VITAL STATS
REAL NAME: Joseph "Robbie" Robertson
OCCUPATION: Reporter, editor-in-chief for *The Daily Bugle*
BASE: New Daily Bugle Building, New York City
HEIGHT: 6 ft 1 in (1.85 m)
WEIGHT: 201 lbs (91.17 kg)
EYES: Brown
HAIR: White
ORIGIN: Human
POWERS: Robbie is a newspaper editor, manager, and reporter. He has wisdom, courage, great integrity and intelligence.

ENERGY PROJECTION	STRENGTH	DURABILITY	FIGHTING SKILL	INTELLIGENCE	SPEED
1	2	2	2	3	2

POWER RANK

...SE

Richard Fisk, son of the criminal Kingpin, is torn between a desire to join his father's underworld empire or overthrow it. Richard takes the identity of the Rose and launches several attempts to topple the family business. Starting a gang war as the "Blood Rose," Richard seemingly dies at his mother's hands.

The Rose didn't rise to his lofty criminal rank without eliminating a few rivals. He could be charming, but was utterly ruthless.

VITAL STATS

REAL NAME: Richard Fisk
OCCUPATION: Crime lord
BASE: Formerly New York City
HEIGHT: 5 ft 10 in (1.78 m)
WEIGHT: 185 lbs (83.91 kg)
EYES: Blue
HAIR: Blond
ORIGIN: Human
POWERS: The Rose took after his father and became a cunning criminal mastermind. He was skilled with most types of firearms.

Richard wore the flower denoting his criminal alias in his lapel.

FEUDING FAMILY
As the Rose, Richard Fisk wore a full-face mask to keep his identity a secret. He soon earned a reputation as an unflappable mastermind. One of his criminal money-spinning rackets—fixing football games—was rumbled by Spider-Man and revealed by *The Daily Bugle.*

Kingpin chose to resurrect Richard using mystical artifacts, believing that it was what his wife would have wanted.

POWER RANK	ENERGY PROJECTION	STRENGTH	DURABILITY	FIGHTING SKILL	INTELLIGENCE	SPEED
	2	2	3	4	3	2

SANDMAN

Sandman and Spider-Man have worked together on occasion, and both have been members of the Outlaws crime-fighting team.

Flint Marko escaped from prison and stumbled on an atomic testing facility. Exposure to radiation turned him into the Sandman. Now composed of living sand and able to shape-shift into any form, the Sandman fought Spider-Man on his own and as a member of the Sinister Six and the Frightful Four, before later making peace with the wall-crawler.

GOOD INTENTIONS
Sandman isn't a bad guy, but in the past he has been driven to rage over his failure to protect Keemia, a little girl he views as his daughter. He has tried to obtain custody of Keemia, and has worked against villains like Doctor Octopus when he thought their actions would put the girl in danger.

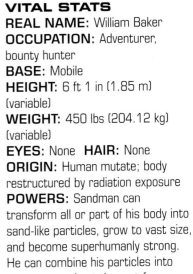

Sandman can control every particle of his body.

William often goes by the alias "Flint Marko."

VITAL STATS
REAL NAME: William Baker
OCCUPATION: Adventurer, bounty hunter
BASE: Mobile
HEIGHT: 6 ft 1 in (1.85 m) (variable)
WEIGHT: 450 lbs (204.12 kg) (variable)
EYES: None **HAIR:** None
ORIGIN: Human mutate; body restructured by radiation exposure
POWERS: Sandman can transform all or part of his body into sand-like particles, grow to vast size, and become superhumanly strong. He can combine his particles into weapons or shoot them at foes.

ENERGY PROJECTION	STRENGTH	DURABILITY	FIGHTING SKILL	INTELLIGENCE	SPEED
1			4	2	2

POWER RANK

SASHA KRAVINOFF

The widow of Kraven the Hunter, Sasha Kravinoff blamed Spider-Man for her husband's death. Her vengeful scheme forced Spider-Man to battle his most dangerous enemies one after the other until he was exhausted, and culminated in a war that Sasha called the "Grim Hunt," after her dead son, Vladimir, alias Grim Hunter.

Sasha brought Kraven back from the grave, but he claimed all she had given him was a corrupt "un-life."

VITAL STATS

REAL NAME: Aleksandra "Sasha" Kravinoff
OCCUPATION: Criminal, assassin
BASE: Mobile
HEIGHT: 5 ft 7 in (1.7 m)
WEIGHT: 136 lbs (61.69 kg)
EYES: Blue **HAIR:** Black
ORIGIN: Human with latent Inhuman lineage
POWERS: Sasha is a cunning criminal and killer who will stop at nothing to get her way. She is also a trained hunter and martial artist.

Sasha would go to any lengths to restore the Kravinoff name and keep her family at the top of the food chain.

RUTHLESS MASTERMIND
Sasha gathered the surviving members of the Kravinoff family, including her daughter Ana and Kraven's villainous half-brother, the Chameleon, in the hope of resurrecting her lost love Kraven the Hunter. She also kidnapped Madame Web and Spider-Woman Mattie Franklin. Her ultimate goal was the death of Spider-Man!

A master of manipulation, Sasha is an implacable opponent.

	ENERGY PROJECTION	STRENGTH	DURABILITY	FIGHTING SKILL	INTELLIGENCE	SPEED
POWER RANK	1	2	2	4	3	2

SCARLET SPIDER BEN REILLY

When Ben Reilly's "clone brother" Kaine uses the Scarlet Spider identity, he favors a red and black suit with red eyes and stealth capability.

Ben Reilly, Peter Parker's clone, believes just as fervently as Peter that with great power must come great responsibility, so he too chooses the path of a hero. Seeking to forge his own life and identity, he becomes Scarlet Spider after the name is coined by a reporter. Although originally created to bring down Spider-Man, Scarlet Spider becomes like a brother to Peter Parker.

Ben Reilly's distinctive Scarlet Spider costume includes a customized blue hoodie.

CLONE RIVALS
Ben Reilly is the longest-standing Scarlet Spider, but fellow Spider-Man clone Kaine has also held the moniker. He uses it as a form of atonement for his past, and chooses to stay in Houston, Texas, rather than return to hero-crowded New York. The two Scarlet Spiders have been bitter enemies in the past, but later learn to work together.

Scarlet Spider wears a utility belt, web-shooters, and a mask, the latter as much for protecting Pater Parker's secret identity as his own.

VITAL STATS
REAL NAME: Benjamin Reilly
OCCUPATION: Super Hero
BASE: New York City
HEIGHT: 5 ft 10 in (1.78 m)
WEIGHT: 165 lbs (75 kg)
EYES: Hazel
HAIR: Brown
ORIGIN: A clone of Peter Parker created by the Jackal (Miles Warren)
POWERS: Ben has Peter Parker's super-strength, speed, stamina, durability, agility, and reflexes. He has the ability to wall-crawl and spider-sense.

ENERGY PROJECTION	STRENGTH	DURABILITY	FIGHTING SKILL	INTELLIGENCE	SPEED
1	4	3	4	4	3

POWER RANK

SCORCHER

Furious when his boss accused him of stealing, chemist Steven Hudak built a suit armed with flamethrowers and, as the Scorcher, set out to burn the business to the ground. Spider-Man stopped the Scorcher, but the villain soon found his services in demand by crime bosses wanting to turn up the heat.

Heat blasts fired by Scorcher will cook Spidey to a crisp if he remains in the line of fire.

VITAL STATS

REAL NAME:
Steven Hudak

OCCUPATION:
Professional criminal;
former chemist

BASE: Mobile

HEIGHT: 5 ft 10 in (1.78 m)

WEIGHT: 175 lbs (79.38 kg)

EYES: Brown

HAIR: None

ORIGIN: Human

POWERS: Scorcher's armored costume gives him superhuman durability and houses powerful flamethrowers. He flies using a jetpack.

Flamethrowers are fed by fuel canisters built into the suit.

Scorcher's suit is completely fireproof— it has to be!

HOT HIRE
Scorcher joined the Hood's criminal army to carry out raids against the Hood's rival, Mr. Negative. This gave Scorcher more opportunities to test himself against Spider-Man. The wall-crawler has proved too fast and agile so far, but Scorcher is determined to send Spidey up in flames.

POWER RANK	ENERGY PROJECTION	STRENGTH	DURABILITY	FIGHTING SKILL	INTELLIGENCE	SPEED
	4	2	3	4	4	3

SCORPIA

Elaine Coll first took on the identity of Scorpia in order to become a weapon for the Maggia crime organization in their war against rival gangs. Equipped with a high-tech suit by the crime lord Silvermane, Scorpia eventually fell into a life as a mercenary and petty criminal in New York City. Inevitably, this brought her into conflict with various protectors of New York, including Daredevil and Spider-Man.

When New York was trapped inside a dome of Darkforce energy, Scorpia found herself teaming up with fellow villain Shocker and the X-Man Rogue to help save the city.

TEAM PLAYER
While usually not the sharing kind, Scorpia has frequently been part of Super Villain team lineups. She has fought alongside the Assassins Guild, the Sinister Seven, and the Syndicate, and got her start as a super-powered villain as part of the powerful organized crime family known as the Maggia.

Arm-mounted "pincers" can fire a range of energy blasts: electrical, laser, microwave, or plasma.

Scorpia's tail can not only "sting" but also crush and slice.

VITAL STATS
REAL NAME: Elaine Coll
OCCUPATION: Super Villain
BASE: New York City
HEIGHT: 5 ft 10 in (1.78 m)
WEIGHT: 140 lbs (63.5 kg)
EYES: Brown
HAIR: Black
ORIGIN: Human
POWERS: Scorpia uses an upgraded version of the suit used by Scorpion (Mac Gargan). It enhances her strength and speed 500 percent and provides protection against mortal injury via a force field. Her tail and pincers can deliver various energy blasts.

ENERGY PROJECTION	STRENGTH	DURABILITY	FIGHTING SKILL	INTELLIGENCE	SPEED
4	4	4	3	2	4

POWER RANK

SCORPION

Transformed by an experimental mutagen, Mac Gargan gained the heightened strength and reflexes of a scorpion, as well as a cybernetic battlesuit with a quick-striking tail. J. Jonah Jameson ordered him to go up against Spider-Man, but the Scorpion couldn't strike a killing blow. Later bonded to a Venom symbiote, then paralyzed by Carnage, Gargan became totally dependent on his Scorpion armor for mobility.

Different versions of Scorpion's battle armor have included built-in weapons and stabbing tail-tips, making him an unpredictable foe for Spider-Man.

VITAL STATS

REAL NAME: Macdonald "Mac" Gargan
OCCUPATION: Advance agent for Alchemax, enforcer for Black Cat's gang
BASE: Alchemax Tower, New York City
HEIGHT: 6 ft 2 in (1.88 m)
WEIGHT: 220 lbs (99.79 kg)
EYES: Brown
HAIR: Shaved
ORIGIN: Human mutate; underwent superhuman augmentation to become the Scorpion
POWERS: Scorpion has the strength and agility of a scorpion grown to human size. His battlesuit has a mechanical tail that can sting, fire electrical blasts, or rocket him into the air.

Scorpion's tail is his most dangerous weapon.

TRYING OUT A NEW LOOK
Mac Gargan later became the new host for the Venom symbiote, and even became a fake "Spider-Man" as a member of Norman Osborn's Dark Avengers team. But the Scorpion role was never far from his heart, and he soon returned to his classic identity.

POWER RANK	ENERGY PROJECTION	STRENGTH	DURABILITY	FIGHTING SKILL	INTELLIGENCE	SPEED
	1	5	5	2	2	3

SCREWBALL

A new arrival on the villain scene, Screwball likes to show off with an elaborate routine of urban gymnastics and spectacular stunts. She makes sure that her exploits are live-streamed on the internet. When Screwball tried to masquerade as Spider-Man, her act came to a quick end when the *real* wall-crawler showed up.

Screwball's fearless gymnastic stunts can even keep her one step ahead of Spider-Man.

PUBLICITY HOUND
Screwball doesn't care about getting money from her high-risk heists, as long as she gets on camera! She has a video crew operating the cameras that track her actions, uploading live footage to the internet and cutting compilation videos of her most outrageous stunts.

Screwball gets a job as production manager on a Hollywood film being made by Mysterio.

Despite her massive online following, Screwball's true identity remains a secret.

VITAL STATS
REAL NAME: Unknown
OCCUPATION: Arms dealer, criminal, entertainer
BASE: Formerly Las Vegas, Nevada
HEIGHT: 5 ft 9 in (1.75 m)
WEIGHT: 132 lbs (59.87 kg)
EYES: Blue
HAIR: Purple
ORIGIN: Human
POWERS: Screwball has no super-powers, but is a superb gymnast and particularly skilled at leaping over rooftops.

ENERGY PROJECTION	STRENGTH	DURABILITY	FIGHTING SKILL	INTELLIGENCE	SPEED
1	2	2	2	2	2

POWER RANK

Scrier belonged to the mysterious Brotherhood of Scrier cult, answering to its chief, Norman Osborn. When the strange Judas Traveller manipulated Spider-Man and his clone Ben Reilly, Scrier stayed close at hand to ensure that everything unfolded according to Norman Osborn's wishes, before slipping back into the shadows.

Spider-Man fought the Brotherhood of Scrier, but its members are easily replaceable if one is defeated or captured.

VITAL STATS

REAL NAME: Scrier
OCCUPATION: Cosmic being
BASE: Hidden temple in the Himalayas
HEIGHT: Unknown
WEIGHT: Unknown
EYES: Red
HAIR: Unknown
ORIGIN: Cosmic being
POWERS: Scrier is a cunning strategist and manipulator of others. He is also a formidable fighter, able to use an array of high-tech weaponry.

Scrier values stealth and prefers to operate from the shadows.

If forced to fight, Scrier makes a devious and dangerous enemy.

DARK CONNECTIONS
Scrier gains his powers from the organization to which he belongs. The Brotherhood has deep ties to international businesses, the criminal underworld, and the political ruling class. The members of the Brotherhood seldom act directly, instead pulling strings from behind the scenes.

POWER RANK

ENERGY PROJECTION	STRENGTH	DURABILITY	FIGHTING SKILL	INTELLIGENCE	SPEED
3	2	2	5	4	2

SHADRAC

The villainous Shadrac is actually Dr. Gregory Herd, a scientific genius who adopted the identity of Override and could control machinery—including Spider-Man's web-shooters—using a cybernetic headset. During an occult ceremony, he later received the supernatural gifts of the demon Shadrac.

In a standoff with police, Shadrac simply laughed at the officers who threatened him with their handguns.

TOO HOT TO HANDLE
Spider-Man first tangled with Shadrac when he called himself Override. During their rematch, the villain had become a being of flame—a state that left him in constant pain. Spider-Man tried to ease Shadrac's suffering, but there appeared to be no cure for his blazing, burning condition.

With his body consumed by flames, Shadrac has a burning grip.

VITAL STATS
REAL NAME: Gregory "Greg" Herd
OCCUPATION: IT researcher, mercenary, bounty hunter
BASE: Mobile
HEIGHT: 5 ft 10 in (1.78 m)
WEIGHT: 170 lbs (77.11 kg)
EYES: None
HAIR: None
ORIGIN: Human possessed by a demon
POWERS: Shadrac can summon and control flames, and manipulate the emotions of others to achieve whatever outcome he desires.

ENERGY PROJECTION	STRENGTH	DURABILITY	FIGHTING SKILL	INTELLIGENCE	SPEED
5	4	2	2	4	2

POWER RANK

SHANG-CHI

One of the best martial artists in the world, Shang-Chi is known as the Master of Kung Fu and is a global champion for good. Tricked by his evil father into becoming an assassin, Shang-Chi rejected that path and worked to bring about his father's downfall instead. Shang-Chi trained Spider-Man in the "Way of the Spider"—a form of unarmed combat.

Shang-Chi and Spider-Man make a formidable pair, combining combat mastery and super-powered agility.

VITAL STATS

REAL NAME: Shang-Chi
OCCUPATION: Supreme Commander of the Five Weapons Society, adventurer, vigilante
BASE: House of the Deadly Hand, Chinatown, New York City
HEIGHT: 5 ft 10 in (1.78 m)
WEIGHT: 175 lbs (79.38 kg)
EYES: Brown
HAIR: Black
ORIGIN: Human
POWERS: Martial arts training gives Shang-Chi amazing control over his body. He can ignore pain and resist drugs or poisons. His chi mastery gives him amazing strength and the ability to dodge bullets.

Shang-Chi studies the weaknesses of his opponents so he knows when best to strike.

TRAINING SPIDER-MAN
Shang-Chi agreed to customize Spider-Man's martial arts style to reflect the wall-crawler's super-powered speed and agility. Shang-Chi's special training gave Spidey an incredible edge when fighting his foes in hand-to-hand combat. The two heroes later teamed up against Mr. Negative, who was smuggling Chinese immigrants into the U.S.

A kick from Shang-Chi can knock out almost any villain.

POWER RANK	ENERGY PROJECTION	STRENGTH	DURABILITY	FIGHTING SKILL	INTELLIGENCE	SPEED
	1	2	2		3	2

After luring Spider-Man into a trap, Shathra injected him with a numbing, paralyzing venom that nearly killed him.

SHATHRA

When Spider-Man met Ezekiel, he learned that he could be the mystical totem of the spider—a revelation that made him a target for Shathra, totem of the spider-wasp! Because spider-wasps are the natural predators of spiders, Shathra forced Spider-Man into a confrontation in which she revealed her true, deadly insect form.

FORCING A SHOWDOWN
Guided by Ezekiel, Spider-Man arranged a rematch deep inside an African temple in order to turn the tables on Shathra. She lost their battle and became prey for the spider creatures that dwelled in the depths of the temple's catacombs.

VITAL STATS
REAL NAME: Shathra
OCCUPATION: Mother to Astral Plane inhabited by spider-wasps.
BASE: Astral Plane
HEIGHT: 6 ft 2 in (1.88 m)
WEIGHT: 120 lbs (54.43 kg)
EYES: White or red
HAIR: Black
ORIGIN: Spider-wasp totem
POWERS: Shathra is a spider-wasp with superhuman strength, speed, agility, and senses. She can teleport, has claws, and can fire sharp stingers.

Shathra's body is covered with sharp spines and stingers.

Shathra can also take on a human form named Sharon Keller.

ENERGY PROJECTION	STRENGTH	DURABILITY	FIGHTING SKILL	INTELLIGENCE	SPEED
3	4	3	4	2	3

POWER RANK

S

S.H.I.E.L.D.

Formed after World War II as the Supreme Headquarters
International Espionage and Law-Enforcement Division,
S.H.I.E.L.D. is a global peacekeeping force that operates
under a code of strict secrecy. S.H.I.E.L.D. is equipped
with high-tech wonders, including flying helicarriers, but
at times has also called upon the help of Spider-Man—
both Peter Parker and Miles Morales.
S.H.I.E.L.D. was dissolved in the aftermath
of the Hydra takeover of the U.S.

KEY MEMBERS

1. Nick Fury Jr.: Infinity Formula-fueled former Army Ranger.

2. Black Widow: One of the world's best secret agents.

3. Hawkeye: Elite marksman, also an Avenger.

4. Maria Hill: Ruthless sometime director of S.H.I.E.L.D.

5. Phil Coulson: Special-ops expert.

UNDER NEW MANAGEMENT
For a brief time, Norman Osborn replaced
S.H.I.E.L.D. with his own sinister agency,
H.A.M.M.E.R. When Osborn used the
forces of H.A.M.M.E.R. to assault Asgard,
the home of Thor, Spider-Man and other
heroes worked to stop the war and
discredit Osborn's organization.

SHOCKER

Safecracker Herman Schultz took his career to the next level by designing a pair of "vibro-smasher" gauntlets that released punches of energized air. He became the Shocker and preyed on armored cars and bank vaults. Spider-Man has stopped him again and again, but the Shocker loves money too much to ever retire.

During an outbreak of a spider-virus in New York City, Shocker grew additional arms—making him twice the threat he was before!

READY AND RELIABLE
Shocker may not defeat Spider-Man often, but he has given the wall-crawler a run for his money. This makes Shocker a valuable criminal henchman, and he is often employed to delay Spider-Man and give another villain enough time to complete a crime.

Padded suit absorbs any damage from his own blasts.

Shocker must brace himself before firing his vibro-smashers.

VITAL STATS
REAL NAME: Herman Schultz
OCCUPATION: Crime lord, assassin
BASE: New York City
HEIGHT: 5 ft 9 in (1.75 m)
WEIGHT: 175 lbs (79.38 kg)
EYES: Brown
HAIR: Brown
ORIGIN: Human
POWERS: Shocker is a gifted engineer who wears a protective, shock-absorbing battlesuit. His gauntlets have "vibro-shock" units that project blasts of compressed air or destructive vibrations.

ENERGY PROJECTION	STRENGTH	DURABILITY	FIGHTING SKILL	INTELLIGENCE	SPEED	POWER RANK
5	2		2	3	2	

IEK

When the alien symbiote Carnage breaks out of prison, he takes fellow inmate Shriek with him. Left damaged by her violent past, she joins Carnage in his rampage across New York City. Stopped by Spider-Man and other heroes, she is incarcerated again, but later escapes to reunite with Carnage. She is totally in his thrall, sacrificing herself for his cult so that her body can be the new host for the Demogoblin.

Shriek seeks thrills at the expense of others, but has shown some affection for her fellow villains Carnage and Carrion.

VITAL STATS

REAL NAME: Frances Louise Barrison
OCCUPATION: Criminal
BASE: Mobile
HEIGHT: 5 ft 8 in (1.73 m)
WEIGHT: 115 lbs (52.16 kg)
EYES: Blue
HAIR: Black
ORIGIN: Mutant
POWERS: Shriek can generate a powerful sonic beam to use as a weapon or to fly. She also possesses Dark Empathy, bringing out the bad side in people with her mind when her left eye shines.

Shriek can use her powers to induce fear and terror in people.

SONIC THREATS

Shriek doesn't care about innocents. When she teams up with Carnage to attack the city, Spider-Man needs to work overtime to save New Yorkers from the physical damage and collapsing buildings triggered by her sonic screams.

POWER RANK	ENERGY PROJECTION	STRENGTH	DURABILITY	FIGHTING SKILL	INTELLIGENCE	SPEED
	5	4	3	2	2	3

SILK

As a young girl, Cindy Moon is bitten by the same radioactive spider as Peter Parker. She develops spider-powers and is trained by spider-totem Ezekiel Sims, but when Ezekiel discovers that Morlun is hunting spider-powered beings, he locks Cindy in a bunker for her own protection. She is imprisoned for ten years before Spider-Man learns of her existence and frees her, whereupon she becomes the hero Silk.

Cindy Moon works for J. Jonah Jameson as a budding reporter, but he unknowingly hires her again when he employs Silk to be his bodyguard.

Silk's first costume was one she made herself using only webbing.

SAME BUT DIFFERENT
Bitten by the same spider, Cindy Moon and Peter Parker share a connection that means they can sense each other anywhere in the Spider-Verse. Their powers are very similar but differ in a few crucial ways: Silk is not as strong, but she has a superior spider-sense, and she can produce her own webbing from her hands.

She can shoot webbing with a barbed tip.

VITAL STATS
REAL NAME: Cindy Moon
OCCUPATION: Super Hero, reporter
BASE: New York City
HEIGHT: 5 ft 7 in (1.7 m)
WEIGHT: 130 lbs (59 kg)
EYES: Brown
HAIR: Black
ORIGIN: Human mutate; bitten by the same spider as Peter Parker
POWERS: Silk has super-strength, speed, stamina, durability, agility, and reflexes. She can wall-crawl, generate and shoot her own webbing, and has an advanced spider-sense.

ENERGY PROJECTION	STRENGTH	DURABILITY	FIGHTING SKILL	INTELLIGENCE	SPEED
1	4	3	3	3	3

POWER RANK

ERMANE

Silvio "Silvermane" Manfredi is the boss of one of the most powerful families in the Maggia crime syndicate, and a perennial foe of Spider-man. Silvermane seemingly died during a battle with Dr. Barton Hamilton who had acquired the Green Goblin's powers, but he later returned, with a cyborg body.

As a cyborg, Silvermane has a new, strong body, fueling his determination to be top dog in the crime world once more.

VITAL STATS

REAL NAME: Silvio Manfredi
OCCUPATION: Crime lord, criminal mastermind
BASE: New York City
HEIGHT: 6 ft 2 in (1.88 m)
WEIGHT: 195 lbs (88.45 kg)
EYES: Blue
HAIR: Silver
ORIGIN: Human cyborg
POWERS: Silvermane has a cybernetic body that gives him superhuman strength, durability, stamina, and speed. He is an excellent shot and a good hand-to-hand fighter.

NEW LEASE ON LIFE
A run-in with Cloak and Dagger left Silvermane near death, but he survived by transferring his organic remains into another robotic body. With his new, silvery body parts, he emerged as one of Spider-Man's greatest foes within the Maggia organization.

Mechanical body is bulletproof and unusually strong.

Silvermane acquired his nickname when his hair went prematurely white.

POWER RANK

ENERGY PROJECTION	STRENGTH	DURABILITY	FIGHTING SKILL	INTELLIGENCE	SPEED
1	4	5	4	2	3

Silver Sable has a number of operatives, but Spider-Man is one of her favorites.

SILVER SABLE

Based in the tiny European country of Symkaria, Silver Sable commands a team of international mercenaries, the Wild Pack. Silver inherited the role from her father, who originally formed the Wild Pack to track down war criminals. She worked closely with Spider-Man when she formed the Outlaws.

Silver Sable is skilled with blades and firearms.

Silver Sable's protective costume does not hinder her natural agility.

PRINCIPLED LEADER
Silver Sable has high-paying clients, but only takes on assignments with aims she deems right and proper. Spider-Man believed that she died while helping him defeat Doctor Octopus and a new incarnation of the Sinister Six.

VITAL STATS
REAL NAME: Silvija Sablinova
OCCUPATION: Monarch of Symkaria, mercenary, owner of Silver Sable International
BASE: Symkaria
HEIGHT: 5 ft 5 in (1.65 m)
WEIGHT: 125 lbs (56.7 kg)
EYES: Blue
HAIR: Silver
ORIGIN: Human
POWERS: Silver Sable is a superb martial artist, gymnast, hand-to-hand combatant, expert markswoman, and swordswoman. She is also a fine leader.

ENERGY PROJECTION	STRENGTH	DURABILITY	FIGHTING SKILL	INTELLIGENCE	SPEED
1	2	2		3	2

POWER RANK

SIN-EATER

The mysterious Sin-Eater killed Spider-Man's friend, NYPD captain Jean DeWolff. A vengeful Spider-Man worked with police detective and former S.H.I.E.L.D. agent Stan Carter to solve her murder and those of other victims in the city—only to see Carter unmasked as the Sin-Eater! Later killed by a SWAT team, Carter was resurrected by Kindred to attack Spider-Man, but was defeated by the web-slinger.

Stan Carter wrongly believed he was acting for the greater good. After his arrest, he still had visions of his vigilante alter-ego.

VITAL STATS

REAL NAME: Stanley "Stan" Carter
OCCUPATION: Killer; former police detective and S.H.I.E.L.D. agent
BASE: New York City
HEIGHT: 5 ft 11 in (1.8 m)
WEIGHT: 170 lbs (77 kg)
EYES: Blue
HAIR: Brown, white at temples
ORIGIN: Human mutate; enhanced by experimental drugs
POWERS: Sin-Eater had police and government training and was an above-average combatant and detective. He had experience with a wide variety of firearms.

Suit conceals Sin-Eater's identity.

Sin-Eater wears a police badge, as he believes his actions are justified.

HIDING IN PLAIN SIGHT
Stan Carter used his S.H.I.E.L.D. training to keep his true nature a secret from his fellow officers on the police force, while using case files to identify his next victims. He didn't target villains, but instead sought out authority figures that he judged had failed in their duties to the public.

POWER RANK

ENERGY PROJECTION	STRENGTH	DURABILITY	FIGHTING SKILL	INTELLIGENCE	SPEED
1	3	2	4	2	2

SINISTER SIX

Doctor Octopus formed the Sinister Six on one principle—strength in numbers! With an original roster of Electro, Kraven the Hunter, Vulture, Mysterio, and Sandman on his side, Doc Ock tried—and failed—to bring about Spidey's ultimate defeat. Later iterations of the Super Villain team had different members, and even different numbers, but Octavius was nearly always a key member.

KEY MEMBERS

1. **Doctor Octopus:** Controls four mechanical arms.

2. **Lizard:** Controls other reptiles telepathically and has razor-sharp teeth.

3. **Electro:** Can generate destructive electrical bolts.

4. **Mysterio:** Able to generate illusions and hallucinations.

5. **Kraven the Hunter:** Physically strong hunter and tracker.

6. **Sandman:** Sand-like body can shape-shift.

Mysterio's gloves and boots emit mind-bending gas.

Curt Connors' Lizard persona had been forcibly separated from his body by Doctor Octopus.

SINISTER COMEBACK

The demonic Kindred manipulated a legion of Super Villains to attack Spider-Man at the same time. Foremost among these was a new Sinister Six, comprising all the original lineup except with Lizard replacing Vulture, who was leading a new Savage Six at the time.

SINISTER SYNDICATE ORIGINAL

Taking inspiration from the Sinister Six, the Beetle recruited Hydro-Man, Boomerang, Speed Demon, the Rhino, and others to form a new villainous team, the Sinister Syndicate. They soon discovered that there was little honor among villains, and infighting—as well as Spider-Man—helped bring about the Syndicate's downfall.

CASH GRABS
Unlike Doctor Octopus' Sinister Six, the Sinister Syndicate was more interested in profiting from crime than getting revenge on Spider-Man. They thought that their Super Villain team-up couldn't fail to make them super-rich, but they reckoned without Spidey.

KEY MEMBERS

1. **Hydro-Man:** Made of living water, he can use his body for attack or escape.

2. **Boomerang:** Skilled at throwing his arsenal of specialty boomerangs.

3. **Rhino:** Incredibly strong and wears a nearly indestructible suit.

4. **Beetle:** Operates a flying armored suit that can fire energy blasts

5. **Speed Demon:** Can run at superhuman speeds.

Team leader Beetle is well-versed in attack strategies.

Rhino is the team's most powerful member.

1. **Beetle (Janice Lincoln):** The leader and founder of the group gains various abilities from her Beetle suit.

2. **Electro (Francine Frye):** Former Super Villain super-fan Frye has absorbed the previous Electro's energy powers.

3. **Lady Octopus:** Genius scientist Carolyn Trainer wields prehensile metal tentacles like those of her mentor Otto Octavius.

4. **Scorpia:** Originally equipped by the Maggia crime family, Scorpia's suit gives her enhanced abilities including a powerful "sting."

5. **Trapstr:** The mysterious Trapstr fires adhesive paste that can immobilize her enemies.

6. **White Rabbit:** The wealthy Lorina Dodson funds the Syndicate and uses a variety of eccentric gadgets to commit crime.

(SINISTER) SYNDICATE NEW

The new iteration of the Sinister Syndicate usually just refer to themselves as "The Syndicate." They are a female-only Super Villain team, founded by Beetle and financed by the White Rabbit, to represent women in the male-dominated field of crime. Unlike some teams, they are a professional outfit, with a mission statement and even a retirement plan. As Spider-Man discovers, they run various "plays" to better utilize the different strengths of each member.

The Syndicate try to be different, but like any villain team-up their unity is threatened by hidden agendas and personal ambition.

SLINGERS

Spider-Man created the alternate identities of Hornet, Ricochet, Dusk, and Prodigy for himself, but when he returned to his original role it fell to four teenagers to inherit Spider-Man's old costumes. As the Slingers, the rookie squad fought evil and tried to live up to the example set by Spider-Man.

Led by Prodigy, the Slingers had a rocky start but grew to trust one another. They now work well as a team.

KEY MEMBERS

Hornet: Suit allows him to fly and fire energy beams.

Prodigy: Suit provides damage resistance and enhanced strength.

Ricochet: Has superhuman agility and the ability to sense danger.

Dusk: Can teleport and form solid constructs made of dark energy.

Ricochet can sense danger nearby in a similar way to Spider-Man.

KEEPING THE FAITH

Before they could work together as a team, the Slingers needed to overcome their suspicions and learn to trust one another. They found a benefactor in the Black Marvel, a retired Super Hero who believed that the Slingers could follow in Spider-Man's footsteps and become heroes for the next generation.

SLYDE

Discovering that he had invented a completely frictionless substance, chemist Jalome Beacher coated a costume with the stuff and became the slippery criminal Slyde. The costume allows Slyde to easily escape from Spider-Man's sticky webbing. After a spell in Pleasant Hill, the top-secret prison where Super Villains believed they were living in an idyllic small town, Slyde returned to help with Chance's evil schemes.

As he got better at using his suit, Slyde introduced new weapons to his arsenal including swords and throwing stars.

Slyde's costume is completely frictionless.

SLIPPERY AS AN EEL
Slyde has a lighthearted attitude toward crime, convinced that his anti-friction technology will allow him to stay one step ahead of the police. Spider-Man has been forced to change his approach when dealing with Slyde, lest the inventive crook use his powers to slip through Spidey's fingers.

Knee pads protect from hard landings.

VITAL STATS
REAL NAME: Jalome Beacher
OCCUPATION: Mercenary, professional criminal
BASE: New York City
HEIGHT: 5 ft 11 in (1.8 m)
WEIGHT: 170 lbs (77.11 kg)
EYES: Brown
HAIR: Black
ORIGIN: Human
POWERS: Former chemical engineer Slyde wears a costume covered with a substance so slippery he can slip through virtually any grasp. He can glide across any surface like he's skating on a frozen lake.

ENERGY PROJECTION	STRENGTH	DURABILITY	FIGHTING SKILL	INTELLIGENCE	SPEED
1	2	2	2	3	2

POWER RANK

SOLO

The independent agent Solo is dedicated to the elimination of international terrorism. Armed and dangerous, Solo also has the ability to teleport directly into combat situations to get the drop on his foes. Solo notably teamed up with Spider-Man to defeat the Sinister Six.

Solo's greatest weapon is his power of teleportation. He can teleport to safety while leaving a grenade behind for his enemies.

VITAL STATS
REAL NAME: James Bourne
OCCUPATION: Mercenary
BASE: Mobile
HEIGHT: 6 ft (1.83 m)
WEIGHT: 200 lbs (90.72 kg)
EYES: Brown
HAIR: Brown
ORIGIN: Human cyborg
POWERS: Solo has Special Forces training in counter-terrorism, and is an expert with various weapons and in forms of hand-to-hand combat. Cybernetic chips in his neck enable him to teleport.

Solo is a big fan of the playwright William Shakespeare.

Armor has light-refractive properties for camouflage.

MAN WITH A MISSION
Solo has rejected his U.S. citizenship so that he can become a truly global force in the fight against terror. He has been a frequent ally of both Spider-Man and the Black Cat, and has lent his services to Nick Fury and the forces of S.H.I.E.L.D.

POWER RANK	ENERGY PROJECTION	STRENGTH	DURABILITY	FIGHTING SKILL	INTELLIGENCE	SPEED
	2	2	5		4	2

It can be tough for opponents to hit Speed Demon, but he is weak against broad-range attacks like Shocker's blasts.

SPEED DEMON

Originally known as the Whizzer, Speed Demon is an old foe of the Avengers, and fought Spider-Man while serving with one of the lineups of the Sinister Syndicate. He also returned to taunt the wall-crawler as part of the Boomerang Revenge Squad. Speed Demon moves so fast he can generate miniature whirlwinds with his body that knock down attackers.

Agile and strong, Speed Demon fights best at super-speed.

Costume reduces friction at high speeds.

THUNDERBOLT THEFT
His frequent defeats at the hands of Spider-Man led Speed Demon to join the team of villains-turned-heroes known as the Thunderbolts. While serving with the Thunderbolts, Speed Demon secretly made money on the side, committing crimes under his Whizzer identity.

VITAL STATS
REAL NAME: James Sanders
OCCUPATION: Adventurer, professional criminal
BASE: Mobile
HEIGHT: 5 ft 11 in (1.8 m)
WEIGHT: 175 lbs (79.38 kg)
EYES: Brown
HAIR: Blond
ORIGIN: Human mutate; given powers by a formula supplied to him by the Grandmaster
POWERS: Speed Demon has superhuman strength, stamina, and durability, but his most notable attribute is his amazing speed. He is also a good hand-to-hand fighter.

ENERGY PROJECTION	STRENGTH	DURABILITY	FIGHTING SKILL	INTELLIGENCE	SPEED
1	3	3	3	3	5

POWER RANK

SPENCER SMYTHE

Scientist Spencer Smythe created a robot called a Spider-Slayer to bring down Spider-Man, and persuaded *Daily Bugle* editor J. Jonah Jameson to use it in a press campaign against the wall-crawler. Spencer's obsession with destroying Spidey led him to create more Spider-Slayers with different powers. He died without achieving his goal, but was given a second chance when he was resurrected as a clone by the Jackal.

Each generation of Smythe's Spider-Slayer robots gained new ways to fight Spider-Man. The wall-crawler was surprised at first, but always won in the end.

VITAL STATS

REAL NAME: Spencer Smythe
OCCUPATION: Roboticist, engineer, inventor
BASE: New York City
HEIGHT: 5 ft 10 in (1.78 m)
WEIGHT: 175 lbs (79.38 kg)
EYES: Gray
HAIR: Gray
ORIGIN: Human
POWERS: Smythe had no super-powers, but was an engineering and robotics genius who tragically used his great gifts for evil purposes.

An elderly man, Spencer was no match for Spidey in a fair fight.

THE SMYTHE LEGACY
Spencer Smythe died due to exposure to radioactive materials used in the construction of the Spider-Slayer robots. Even though he brought about his own demise, Spencer blamed his sickness on others. His son Alistair took up his father's vendetta and continued the construction of Spider-Slayer robots.

POWER RANK

ENERGY PROJECTION	STRENGTH	DURABILITY	FIGHTING SKILL	INTELLIGENCE	SPEED
1	2	2	1	5	2

As Spider-Girl, Anya soon became a fixture in the New York Super Hero scene, and sometimes teamed up with Spider-Man.

SPIDER-GIRL

Anya Corazon gained mystic abilities when the Spider Society chose her as their hunter and charged her with the responsibility of battling the Society's enemies in the Sisterhood of the Wasp. Anya later rejected the Spider Society and the name it had given her, Araña, becoming the first hero to take the name Spider-Girl. She became a founding member of the spider-powered team the Order of the Web.

EARNING HER NAME
After enduring an ordeal in which Charlotte Witter stole the abilities of every spider-powered woman, Anya emerged with a new costume and identity. As she learned what it took to live up to the name Spider-Girl, Anya sought advice from other heroes.

Anya is proud to wear the spider symbol.

Anya is a founding member of the Order of the Web.

VITAL STATS
REAL NAME: Aña "Anya" Sofia Corazon
OCCUPATION: High School student
BASE: New York City
HEIGHT: 5 ft 3 in (1.6 m)
WEIGHT: 115 lbs (52.16 kg)
EYES: Brown
HAIR: Brown
ORIGIN: Human augmented by magic
POWERS: A magical, spider-shaped tattoo gives Anya powers similar to Spider-Man's. She can generate her own webs from glands in her arms. She has received combat training from S.H.I.E.L.D.

ENERGY PROJECTION	STRENGTH	DURABILITY	FIGHTING SKILL	INTELLIGENCE	SPEED
1	4	5	4	2	3

POWER RANK

SPIDER-HAM

When the disoriented and irradiated pig scientist May Porker bites a spider after an experiment goes wrong, she triggers the spider's transformation into a humanoid pig with the powers of a spider. May's scientific genius was also transferred during the fateful bite. Peter Porker, the "Spectacular Spider-Ham" as he calls himself, uses his newfound abilities to fight crime, and is part of the Spider-Army assembled to battle the Inheritors.

Peter Porker occasionally works with other animal heroes in his reality, although they find his brash attitude and inappropriate jokes annoying.

VITAL STATS
REAL NAME: Peter Porker
OCCUPATION: Super Hero
BASE: New Yolk City, Earth-8311
HEIGHT: 5 ft 2 in (1.57 m)
WEIGHT: 95 lbs (43 kg)
EYES: Black
HAIR: Brown
ORIGIN: A spider named Peter who was bitten by a radioactive pig; he transformed into an anthropomorphic pig but retains the proportionate strength and speed of a spider.
POWERS: Spider-Ham has super-strength, speed, durability, stamina, reflexes, and agility. He can wallcrawl and possesses a spider-sense.

Spider-Ham has a "spider-nonsense"—he becomes more cartoony the more danger he senses.

CARTOON PHYSICS
As a being from the cartoon world of Earth-8311, Spider-Ham is not bound by the same laws of physics as most of the multiverse. He can stretch and reshape his body, withstand massive surges of electricity, and produce oversized mallets seemingly from nowhere when fighting opponents.

Having lost his natural web-spinning ability during his transformation, Peter builds his own wrist-mounted web-shooters.

POWER RANK	ENERGY PROJECTION	STRENGTH	DURABILITY	FIGHTING SKILL	INTELLIGENCE	SPEED
	1	4	4	4	4	3

SPIDERLING

Annie May Parker is the daughter of Peter Parker and Mary Jane Watson Parker on Earth-18119. She inherits spider-powers from her father, although with a slight difference—her spider-sense is so strong that it resembles premonition of future events. Although at first her parents seek to protect Annie from the life of a Super Hero, they finally accept that she wants to protect people as Spider-Man does.

Annie manipulates the Web of Life and Destiny into armor for herself and her allies, Anya Corazon (Spider-Girl of Earth-616) and Mayday Parker (Spider-Woman of Earth-982).

THE PATTERNMAKER
Annie is one of the most important spider-totems in the Spider-Verse. As the Patternmaker, she has the power to navigate and remake the threads of the Web of Life and Destiny. When the Web is destroyed by an alternate-reality Norman Osborn, it falls to Annie to create a new one.

To protect her as a child, Annie's parents fitted her with an inhibitor chip coded to her DNA to suppress her powers.

Spiderling wears wrist-mounted web-spinners that enable her to trap opponents or travel by web-swinging.

VITAL STATS
REAL NAME: Anna May "Annie" Parker
OCCUPATION: Super Hero; student
BASE: Earth-001; formerly Earth-18119
HEIGHT: 5 ft 5 in (1.65 m)
WEIGHT: 118 lbs (54 kg)
EYES: Green
HAIR: Red
ORIGIN: Inherited spider-powers from her father, the Peter Parker of Earth-18119
POWERS: Spiderling has super strength, speed, durability, stamina, reflexes, and agility. She can wall-crawl and has an enhanced premonition-like spider-sense.

ENERGY PROJECTION	STRENGTH	DURABILITY	FIGHTING SKILL	INTELLIGENCE	SPEED
1	4	3	4	4	3

POWER RANK

SPIDER-MAN NOIR

Peter Parker lives in New York City, Earth-90214, in a country devastated by the Great Depression. He sees the terrible consequences of poverty every day in his job as a reporter for *The Daily Bugle*, so when he gains mysterious powers after being bitten by a spider, he becomes a champion of the downtrodden—the Spider-Man.

Despite being very much a lone operator in his home reality, the Spider-Man becomes a key member of the multiversal Web-Warriors.

VITAL STATS

REAL NAME: Peter Parker
OCCUPATION: Super Hero, reporter
BASE: New York City, Earth-90214
HEIGHT: 5 ft 10 in (1.78 m)
WEIGHT: 174 lbs (79 kg)
EYES: Brown
HAIR: Brown
ORIGIN: Human mutate; bitten by a spider that had come to America in a crate of rare antiquities
POWERS: Peter Parker has super-strength, speed, durability, stamina, reflexes, and agility. He can shoot organic webbing from his wrists, has a spider-sense, and can wall-crawl.

The Spider-Man can make and shoot web-fluid from his own body; he does not need web-shooters.

ANCIENT MYSTERIES
The Spider-Man of Earth-90214 has powers that seem to owe more to mystical forces than to science. He is empowered by the "Spider-God" Ereshkigal, who is connected to the Web of Life and Destiny. Ereshkigal is even able to resurrect the Spider-Man from the dead.

The Spider-Man's costume was made from a repurposed pilot's uniform worn by his uncle Ben in World War I.

POWER RANK	ENERGY PROJECTION	STRENGTH	DURABILITY	FIGHTING SKILL	INTELLIGENCE	SPEED
	1	3	4	4	4	3

SPIDER-MAN 2099

The Spider-Man of 2099 had a rocky run-in with the Spider-Man of the modern era during a time-travel adventure.

In the distant future of 2099, scientist Miguel O'Hara gained super-powers, including the ability to scale walls with his finger-talons and a venomous bite. Inspired by the Spider-Man he had seen in historical records, Miguel donned a similar costume to battle villains as the Spider-Man of his era.

Streamlined costume allows for fluid movements.

The Spider-Man of 2099 shares his predecessor's speed and agility.

PAST ADVENTURES
In order to prevent his timeline from being erased, the Spider-Man of 2099 traveled backward in history, teaming up with the Spider-Man of the present day. His mission? To protect the life of his own grandfather and make sure that Miguel O'Hara is born on schedule!

VITAL STATS
REAL NAME: Miguel O'Hara
OCCUPATION: Retired adventurer, businessman, scientist, vigilante
BASE: Nueva York, Earth-928
HEIGHT: 5 ft 10 in (1.78 m)
WEIGHT: 170 lbs (77.11 kg)
EYES: Red
HAIR: Brown
ORIGIN: Human mutate; gained powers in a laboratory accident
POWERS: Miguel has similar powers to Spider-Man's. He also has fangs and razor-sharp claws, and can move so fast he leaves a body double behind, confusing foes.

ENERGY PROJECTION	STRENGTH	DURABILITY	FIGHTING SKILL	INTELLIGENCE	SPEED
2	4	3	2	4	4

POWER RANK

SPIDER-PUNK

Hobie Brown lives in New York City, Earth-138, where an apathetic population is dominated by mega-corporations. He expresses his rage against the authorities through music, playing punk rock with his band, the Spider-Slayers. When not playing music, Hobie, who got powers from a radioactive spider bite, is the vigilante and rebel Spider-Punk, although he prefers to go by the name Spider-Man.

Spider-Punk is in his element when he is called upon to jam with Earth-65's Gwen Stacy so that they can harness energy to repair the Web of Life and Destiny.

VITAL STATS

REAL NAME: Hobie Brown
OCCUPATION: Super Hero, musician
BASE: New York City, Earth-138
HEIGHT: 5 ft 11 in (1.8 m)
WEIGHT: 150 lbs (68 kg)
EYES: Brown
HAIR: Black
ORIGIN: Human mutate; gained spider-powers after being bitten by a radioactive spider as a result of illegal dumping of toxic waste
POWERS: Hobie has super-strength, speed, stamina, durability, agility, and reflexes. He can also wall-crawl and has a spider-sense.

Hobie Brown's Spider-Man costume reflects his punk aesthetic, with head spikes and a denim vest.

ANARCHIC SPIDER-MAN
Spider-Punk's downtrodden world has made him more brutal than a lot of spider-heroes. His anger and unpredictability makes him an ideal recruit for the Superior Spider-Man's (Otto Octavius) Spider-Army as he attempts to take on the Inheritors. Surprisingly, Hobie takes to teamwork and goes on to be a member of the Web-Warriors.

As well as his spider-powers, Spider-Punk has been known to use his guitars as effective weapons.

POWER RANK	ENERGY PROJECTION	STRENGTH	DURABILITY	FIGHTING SKILL	INTELLIGENCE	SPEED
	1	4	3	4	2	3

SPIDER-SLAYERS

Advanced models of Spider-Slayers incorporate self-repairing metals and nanotechnology.

Built by Spencer Smythe and later by his son Alistair, Spider-Slayer robots come in all shapes and sizes and are programmed to hunt, capture, and destroy Spider-Man. Most Spider-Slayers have smooth surfaces that resist Spider-Man's webbing, and can fire sticky webs of their own.

This robot can be controlled remotely or operated by a human pilot.

UPGRADED
Spencer and Alistair also built Spider-Slayers that could be piloted by human operators, to give themselves a chance to inflict what they believed would be Spider-Man's final defeat. Time after time Spider-Man overcame their fearsome technological know-how.

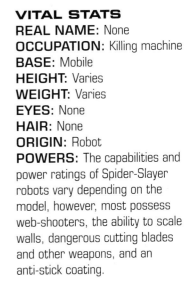

Spider-Man's powers are copied by the Spider-Slayer robots.

VITAL STATS
REAL NAME: None
OCCUPATION: Killing machine
BASE: Mobile
HEIGHT: Varies
WEIGHT: Varies
EYES: None
HAIR: None
ORIGIN: Robot
POWERS: The capabilities and power ratings of Spider-Slayer robots vary depending on the model, however, most possess web-shooters, the ability to scale walls, dangerous cutting blades and other weapons, and an anti-stick coating.

SPIDER-UK

Spider-UK is from Earth-833, where he is not only that reality's Spider Hero but also a member of the Captain Britain Corps. He is given the power of multiversal travel so that he can investigate the killings of spider-totems by the Inheritors. As one of the first to face this existential threat, Spider-UK is a key member of the Spider-Army and later leads the Web-Warriors with notable heroism and supreme sacrifice.

When Spider-UK's reality is destroyed, he pledges to remain at the Web of Life and Destiny and use it to help any worlds without spider-heroes.

VITAL STATS

REAL NAME: Billy Braddock
OCCUPATION: Super Hero
BASE: Earth-833
HEIGHT: 6 ft 1 in (1.85 m)
WEIGHT: 196 lbs (89 kg)
EYES: Blue
HAIR: Brown
ORIGIN: Human mutate; bitten by radioactive spider, which also granted powers as his reality's version of Captain Britain
POWERS: Billy has super-strength, speed, stamina, durability, reflexes, and agility. He can also wall-crawl.

Spider-UK usually wears a device given to him at the mystic Starlight Citadel so that he can travel between dimensions.

CAPTAIN BRITAIN CORPS

Spider-UK is a member of the Captain Britain Corps, an organization of versions of Captain Britain from across the multiverse, brought together by Merlyn and his daughter Roma to protect their respective realities. Later, Spider-UK is filled with guilt and grief when his reality is destroyed while he is away.

Unlike many other spider-powered beings, Spider-UK has no spider-sense of impending danger.

POWER RANK	ENERGY PROJECTION	STRENGTH	DURABILITY	FIGHTING SKILL	INTELLIGENCE	SPEED
	2	4	3	4	4	3

SPIDER-WOMAN JESSICA DREW

The first Spider-Woman started out as an agent of the sinister Hydra organization before devoting herself to heroism. In her civilian identity, Jessica Drew worked as a private investigator. Her unique Spider-Woman powers included the ability to fire electrical "venom blasts."

Jessica Drew's venom blasts are a potent offensive weapon against nearby enemies.

WHO IS THE TRUE SPIDER-WOMAN
Jessica fell victim to the Skrulls, a species of alien shape-changers, who imprisoned her and impersonated her as Spider-Woman within the ranks of the New Avengers. When she escaped, Jessica had to work overtime to regain the trust of her teammates.

Jessica's costume has a distinctive red-and-yellow pattern.

VITAL STATS
REAL NAME: Jessica Miriam "Jess" Drew
OCCUPATION: Adventurer, mercenary, vigilante
BASE: New York City
HEIGHT: 5 ft 10 in (1.78 m)
WEIGHT: 130 lbs (58.97 kg)
EYES: Green
HAIR: Brown (dyed black)
ORIGIN: Human mutate; Jessica was given a life-saving serum made from rare spiders
POWERS: Jessica has abilities similar to Spider-Man. Trained in armed and unarmed combat, she can discharge venom blasts from her hands and fly.

ENERGY PROJECTION	STRENGTH	DURABILITY	FIGHTING SKILL	INTELLIGENCE	SPEED
5	5	4	4	3	3

POWER RANK

ER-WOMAN JULIA CARPENTER

The second person to go by the name of Spider-Woman, Julia Carpenter was a government test subject who struck out on her own to become a Super Hero. In addition to her spider-powers, she can spin a "psi-web" of pure energy. After the death of the previous Madame Web, Julia inherited the mantle, giving her a special connection to the Web of Life and Destiny. She also founded the Order of the Web, a team of spider-powered heroes.

At one point, Julia Carpenter gave up being a Super Hero to look after her daughter, Rachel.

VITAL STATS

REAL NAME: Julia Eugenia Cornwall Carpenter
OCCUPATION: Adventurer
BASE: Mobile
HEIGHT: 5 ft 9 in (1.75 m)
WEIGHT: 140 lbs (63.5 kg)
EYES: Blue
HAIR: Strawberry blond
ORIGIN: Human mutate; injected with experimental mixture containing spider venom.
POWERS: Julia Carpenter has superhuman strength, speed, stamina, and senses, and can wall-crawl like Spider-Man. She can create psi-webs with her mind and later gains the gift of future sight.

BIG CHANGES
After Julia Carpenter gained the future-sight powers of Madame Web, she became an big presence in Spider-Man's life. When Spidey temporarily lost his spider-sense ability, Julia stepped in to help him foresee major events that could threaten his loved ones.

After she became Madame Web, Julia gave her old Spider-Woman costume to Anya Corazon (Spider-Girl).

When Julia became Madame Web she lost her sight but gained the ability of precognition.

POWER RANK

ENERGY PROJECTION	STRENGTH	DURABILITY	FIGHTING SKILL	INTELLIGENCE	SPEED
4	4	3	3	2	3

SPIDER-WOMAN
MATTIE FRANKLIN

Mattie had a playful, flirty character, as Peter Parker occasionally discovered.

Spider-Woman Mattie Franklin had the unique ability to sprout powerful spider legs from her back. Her promising career as Spider-Woman was tragically cut short when the heirs of Kraven the Hunter sacrificed her to resurrect one of their own. She was later brought back as a clone by the Jackal, but succumbed to the Carrion virus in the act of saving the hero Silk from a horde of zombies.

Speed and agility were two of Spider-Woman's greatest gifts.

MATTIE'S FINAL BATTLE
Mattie gained her powers during a mystic ceremony known as the Gathering of the Five. She seemingly lost her life in a similar ceremony, when the villainous Sasha Kravinoff determined that her sacrifice would allow Sasha's husband, Kraven the Hunter, to walk the Earth once more.

Mattie also had the ability to fire out energy blasts from her hands.

VITAL STATS
REAL NAME: Martha "Mattie" Franklin
OCCUPATION: Adventurer
BASE: New York City
HEIGHT: 5 ft 8 in (1.73 m)
WEIGHT: 123 lbs (55.79 kg)
EYES: Blue
HAIR: Black
ORIGIN: Human mutate; powers bestowed in a mystic ritual
POWERS: Mattie's superhuman strength, reflexes, and durability were magic-based. She also briefly absorbed the powers of others who had donned the mantle of Spider-Woman.

ENERGY PROJECTION	STRENGTH	DURABILITY	FIGHTING SKILL	INTELLIGENCE	SPEED
1	4	5	2	3	3

POWER RANK

SPIDER-WOMAN MAY PARKER

In a future timeline, the daughter of Peter Parker and Mary Jane Watson carries on the family legacy as Spider-Woman! With her injured father retired from the dangerous business of crime-fighting, May "Mayday" Parker secretly fights second-generation spider-villains while trying to live the life of a normal teenager.

In her near-future timeline, Spider-Girl swings freely though New York City.

VITAL STATS
REAL NAME: May "Mayday" Parker
OCCUPATION: Super Hero, student, vigilante
BASE: New York City, Earth-982
HEIGHT: 5 ft 7 in (1.7 m)
WEIGHT: 119 lbs (53.98 kg)
EYES: Blue
HAIR: Brown
ORIGIN: Human mutate; inherited her powers from her father, Peter Parker
POWERS: As Peter Parker's daughter, May has superhuman strength, agility stamina, and durability similar to Spider-Man's.

Spider-Woman wears the same mask that her father made famous.

HER OWN HERO
May Parker developed her powers at age 15. In her time as Spider-Girl May has fought a new Green Goblin—the grandson of the original—as well as battling Carnage after the alien symbiote attached itself to one of her high school friends.

May wears her Spider-Woman costume under her school clothes in case adventure calls.

POWER RANK	ENERGY PROJECTION	STRENGTH	DURABILITY	FIGHTING SKILL	INTELLIGENCE	SPEED
	1	4	3	3	2	3

SPINNERET

Mary Jane Watson-Parker is a big believer in the motto "family first." Having brought up a super-powered daughter together with her super-powered husband, she wanted to play just as big a role in protecting their family as anyone else. Using technology liberated from a Super Villain's lair, her husband built her a suit that would mimic his powers and enable her to swing into action as Spinneret.

When Mary Jane decided to try a new suit provided by Allan Biotech, she discovered that it was the Venom symbiote.

Spinneret's suit is originally reverse-engineered by her husband from tech used by the Super Villain Regent.

Like their daughter, Spiderling, Spinneret uses web-shooters and web-fluid designed by Spider-Man (Peter Parker).

POWER DRAIN
Spinneret's original suit got its powers by siphoning them from Peter Parker, occasionally weakening him at crucial moments. Searching for a solution, Mary Jane first had an ill-fated run-in with a Venom suit before being given an all-new costume by Tony Stark.

VITAL STATS
REAL NAME: Mary Jane Watson-Parker
OCCUPATION: Super Hero, boutique owner
BASE: New York City, Earth-18119
HEIGHT: 5 ft 8 in (1.73 m)
WEIGHT: 135 lbs (61 kg)
EYES: Green
HAIR: Red
ORIGIN: Human; given a suit by her husband Peter Parker that bestows his powers on her so that she can protect their daughter Annie
POWERS: When wearing the Spinneret suit, Mary Jane has super-strength, speed, stamina, durability, reflexes, and agility, and can wall-crawl.

ENERGY PROJECTION	STRENGTH	DURABILITY	FIGHTING SKILL	INTELLIGENCE	SPEED
1	4	3	3	2	3

POWER RANK

While researching teleportation technology for the Kingpin, scientist Johnathan Ohnn discovered how to create movable space-warp portals. By carrying the portals on his costume as the Spot, he leaped into a life of crime. When the Spot places his spots around a target, he can attack from many directions at once.

Spot makes use of his teleportation portals during combat and turns Spidey's punch on himself.

VITAL STATS

REAL NAME: Johnathan Ohnn
OCCUPATION: Criminal, thief; former scientist
BASE: New York City
HEIGHT: 5 ft 10 in (1.78 m)
WEIGHT: 170 lbs (77.11 kg)
EYES: Blue
HAIR: Brown
ORIGIN: Human mutate; a lab experiment projected Jonathan Ohnn into the Spotworld dimension.
POWERS: Spot is the living embodiment of the Spotworld dimension; the spots on his body are dimensional portals.

Each teleporting spot can be detached and placed on a surface.

TARGET: SPIDER-MAN
The Spot is usually a loner, but he joined with other villains as a member of the short-lived Spider-Man Revenge Squad. Spot's original goal was to gain cash from robbery, but long exposure to the strange energies given off by his teleportation portals has begun to alter his mind, making his motives hard to predict.

Spot does not trigger the spider-sense of spider-powered heroes.

POWER RANK	ENERGY PROJECTION	STRENGTH	DURABILITY	FIGHTING SKILL	INTELLIGENCE	SPEED
	1	2	3	2	5	2

SQUID

Thug Don Callahan underwent treatments that allowed him to transform at will into a tentacled humanoid squid. As the Squid, he sold his services to local crime bosses and encountered Spider-Man. The Squid lurks in sewers and, when cornered, has a variety of squid defenses.

The Squid is easily led and has been recruited into many Super Villain teams, including the Masters of Evil, the All-New Sinister Six, and the Wicked Brigade.

The Squid's powerful, crushing tentacles are tricky to escape—even for Spider-Man.

SECOND-RATE FOE
Spider-Man doesn't take the Squid very seriously. During their first meeting, Spidey dismissed the new villain for his animal-themed gimmick and his ink-squirting powers. The Squid has tried to earn respect ever since.

VITAL STATS
REAL NAME: Donald Callahan
OCCUPATION: Criminal
BASE: New York City
HEIGHT: 5 ft 9 in (1.75 m)
WEIGHT: 160 lbs (72.57 kg)
EYES: White
HAIR: None
ORIGIN: Human mutate; a criminal organization convinced Donald to undergo an experimental procedure
POWERS: The Squid is able to shift from human form to squid form. His super-strong tentacles are used for attack, and his ink spray is a defensive weapon.

Slippery, flexible body is difficult to damage.

ENERGY PROJECTION	STRENGTH	DURABILITY	FIGHTING SKILL	INTELLIGENCE	SPEED
1	3	3	2	2	2

POWER RANK

175

‡RON

Genetic researcher Vincent Stegron injected his own body with dinosaur DNA and transformed himself into an orange, stegosaurus-like humanoid, complete with a tough hide and incredible physical strength. Stegron is obsessed with the Savage Land—the one place on Earth where mighty dinosaurs still roam.

One of Stegron's ambitions is to turn everyone in the world into a dinosaur-human hybrid and then rule over them all.

VITAL STATS

REAL NAME: Vincent Stegron
OCCUPATION: Scientist, geneticist, engineer, inventor
BASE: Savage Land, Antarctica
HEIGHT: 6 ft 2 in (1.88 m) (as dinosaur); 5 ft 8 in (1.73 m) (as human)
WEIGHT: 350 lbs (158.76 kg) (as dinosaur); 150 lbs (68.04 kg) (as human)
EYES: Green (as dinosaur); Brown (as human)
HAIR: None (as dinosaur); Brown (as human)
ORIGIN: Human mutate; transformed by dinosaur DNA
POWERS: Stegron has superhuman strength, reflexes, and speed, as well as a prehensile, spiky tail to grasp objects or use as a weapon. He can control other dinosaurs with his mind.

Plates on his back give Stegron additional protection.

REPTILES ON A RAMPAGE
Stegron forced Dr. Curt Connors to restore dinosaurs to life using the remains found in a New York City museum. Dr. Connors then transformed into the Lizard and attacked Stegron, forcing Spider-Man to work overtime to contain the damage caused by the two reptilian combatants.

His thick hide cannot be pierced by most weapons.

POWER RANK	ENERGY PROJECTION	STRENGTH	DURABILITY	FIGHTING SKILL	INTELLIGENCE	SPEED
	1	4	5	2	5	3

STILT-MAN

Stilt-Man's battlesuit provides enhanced strength and encases him in a bulletproof shell, though he is still vulnerable to getting knocked off balance.

Stilt-Man Wilbur Day is famous for his unique armored battlesuit. The suit's extendible legs allow Stilt-Man to reach the upper stories of the city's highest skyscrapers, but also leaves him vulnerable to tripping—a flaw frequently exploited by both Spider-Man and Daredevil.

The suit also contains an arsenal of weapons.

LONG-LEGGED LOSER
Despite his talents, Stilt-Man considers himself a failure due to his unremarkable criminal career. Spider-Man thinks Stilt-Man is an engineering genius and is wasting his potential by focusing on lofty stunts, but is always ready to put a stop to his dangerous rampages.

When fully extended, Stilt-Man is taller than a 25-story building.

VITAL STATS
REAL NAME: Wilbur Day
OCCUPATION: Settler; former professional criminal, scientist
BASE: Megiddo
HEIGHT: 5 ft 6 in (1.68 m); 292 ft (89 m) (maximum with battlesuit)
WEIGHT: 150 lbs (68.04 kg); 400 lbs (181.44 kg) (with battlesuit)
EYES: Blue
HAIR: Gray
ORIGIN: Human
POWERS: The legs of Stilt-Man's armored, hydraulic suit can extend to hundreds of feet, and can also be used as battering rams. His suit enhances his strength, durability, and speed.

ENERGY PROJECTION	STRENGTH	DURABILITY	FIGHTING SKILL	INTELLIGENCE	SPEED
3	4	4	3	4	3

POWER RANK

SUE RICHARDS

Sue Richards, aka the Invisible Woman, is the most powerful member of the Fantastic Four. The sister of Johnny Storm (the Human Torch), Sue married Reed Richards (Mister Fantastic). She welcomed Spider-Man into the Fantastic Four during its brief time as the Future Foundation.

Sue is the most constant member in the Fantastic Four's changing lineup, giving her a depth of experience at dealing with trouble that no other member can match.

VITAL STATS

REAL NAME: Susan "Sue" Storm Richards

OCCUPATION: Adventurer

BASE: 4 Yancy Street, New York City

HEIGHT: 5 ft 6 in (1.68 m)

WEIGHT: 120 lbs (54.43 kg)

EYES: Blue

HAIR: Blond

ORIGIN: Human mutate; exposed to cosmic radiation

POWERS: As Invisible Woman, Sue can make herself or other objects invisible and project invisible force fields that can also enable her to fly.

The unstable molecules in Sue's costume allow it to change its appearance.

FAMILY TOGETHERNESS
The Invisible Woman is the person who unites the often-bickering members of the Fantastic Four. She is quick to accept others into the fold and has long viewed Spider-Man as a friend of the family. Sue recommended Spidey for her husband Reed Richards's Future Foundation, a think tank seeking a better future for the world.

Sue can become completely invisible at will.

POWER RANK	ENERGY PROJECTION	STRENGTH	DURABILITY	FIGHTING SKILL	INTELLIGENCE	SPEED
	5	2	5	3	3	3

SUN GIRL

When the Superior Spider-Man's arrogance leads him to make an almost fatally bad judgment, it is Sun Girl who saves him—and New York City.

Selah Burke is a student, whose father is scientist and inventor Dr. Edward Lansky. Inspired by Spider-Man, Selah uses some of her dad's designs to build herself a suit so that she can be a hero too—the light-wielding Sun Girl. However, Sun Girl does not realize that her father is also the villain Lightmaster—that is, until she faces him in battle.

Sun Girl's wings glow as she flies using light-generation technology.

SUPERIOR SUN GIRL
Sun Girl meets and teams up with Spider-Man, unaware that he is Otto Octavius in Peter Parker's body. Although she is disappointed in his attitude, the Superior Spider-Man takes a shine to Sun Girl and uses his genius to upgrade her weaponry.

VITAL STATS
REAL NAME: Selah Burke
OCCUPATION: Super Hero
BASE: New York City
HEIGHT: 5 ft 8 in (1.77 m)
WEIGHT: 130 lbs (59 kg)
EYES: Brown
HAIR: Black
ORIGIN: Human; daughter of villain Lightmaster, she uses his designs to build her own equipment and become a hero.
POWERS: Selah's suit, wrist gauntlets, and wing pack use light-generating technology to enable her to fly and fire offensive laser blasts.

Sun Girl's wrist gauntlets fire powerful laser blasts.

ENERGY PROJECTION	STRENGTH	DURABILITY	FIGHTING SKILL	INTELLIGENCE	SPEED
5	2	2	3	3	3

POWER RANK

SUPERIOR SPIDER-MAN

The Superior Spider-Man was created when Doctor Octopus (Otto Octavius) managed to transfer his consciousness into Peter Parker's body. Octavius vowed to be a better hero than Spider-Man ever was, by using his genius and ruthlessness to put down for good all the villains that had plagued Peter Parker. Superior Spider-Man's brand of "heroics" saw him pull no punches in his battles against the criminals of first New York City, then San Francisco.

Otto Octavius drew on all the tech he had built as a Super Villain to help his new war on crime as the Superior Spider-Man. This included repurposing his Octobots as Spider-Bots.

VITAL STATS

REAL NAME: Otto Octavius/ "Elliot Tolliver"
OCCUPATION: Super Villain turned sometime Super Hero
BASE: New York City; San Francisco
HEIGHT: 5 ft 10 in (1.78 m)
WEIGHT: 167 lbs (75.75 kg)
EYES: Hazel **HAIR:** Brown
ORIGIN: Doctor Octopus transferred his consciousness into the body of Peter Parker
POWERS: Octavius inherited Peter Parker's spider-powers including his wall-crawling ability and spider-sense; also super-strength, speed, agility, stamina, and durability. He retained his genius intellect.

Superior Spider-Man's costume is similar to the original's, but uses black instead of blue.

Octavius introduces various tech upgrades to the suit during his time as Spider-Man, like mechanical spider-arms, HUD goggles, and an AI.

BODY SWAPS
When Peter Parker regained control of his body, Doctor Octopus managed to move his mind to the robot Living Brain. Later he developed a clone hybrid of himself and Peter Parker. He would inhabit this body as Elliot Tolliver, the alter-ego of a new Superior Spider-Man.

POWER RANK

	ENERGY PROJECTION	STRENGTH	DURABILITY	FIGHTING SKILL	INTELLIGENCE	SPEED
	1	4	3	4	5	3

SWARM

Former Nazi scientist Fritz von Meyer came to a bad end when the killer bees he studied turned on him. Somehow his consciousness survived, and he lived on as the swarm's guiding intelligence. Swarm views Spider-Man as a predator of insects, so considers him his natural enemy.

Driven mad over the decades, Swarm hopes to reclaim his former glory using the insects he controls with his mind.

When Swarm attacks, Spider-Man had better stay on the move.

HIVE OF EVIL
Resurrected during a science experiment at Empire State University, Swarm attacked the campus with his legions of killer bees. Peter Parker changed into his Spider-Man costume to battle the threat, only succeeding when he unleashed a chemical concoction that resembled insect repellent.

Swarm's true body is merely a skeleton.

VITAL STATS
REAL NAME: Fritz von Meyer
OCCUPATION: Toxicologist, apiculturist
BASE: Mobile
HEIGHT: 6 ft 5 in (1.96 m)
WEIGHT: 104 lbs (47.17 kg)
EYES: Yellow
HAIR: None
ORIGIN: Human who was consumed by bees
POWERS: Swarm's body is made up of thousands of bees and, controlled by von Meyer's formidable intelligence, can take any shape. Swarm can control bees and other insects.

ENERGY PROJECTION	STRENGTH	DURABILITY	FIGHTING SKILL	INTELLIGENCE	SPEED
1	1		2	2	3

POWER RANK

TARANTULA

As the Tarantula, Anton Miguel Rodriquez worked as an assassin for the rulers of the tyrannical regime ruling his South American homeland of Delvadia. He was sent to the United States to hunt down those that opposed the Delvadian government. His cruel actions led to clashes with Spider-Man.

Tarantula teamed up with other villains to attack Spidey when he was powerless. Luckily, Spidey got his powers back!

VITAL STATS

REAL NAME: Anton Miguel Rodriquez
OCCUPATION: Professional criminal
BASE: New York City
HEIGHT: 6 ft 1 in (1.85 m)
WEIGHT: 185 lbs (83.91 kg)
EYES: Brown
HAIR: Black
ORIGIN: Human
POWERS: Tarantula's military training gave him fighting skills that were later enhanced by drugs. His boots were fitted with blades coated with a poison that could paralyze or kill.

Tarantula's retractable boot spikes are venomous.

Spidey has to beware Tarantula's deadly touch.

POWERING UP
Tarantula originally had no super-powered abilities, but he was injected with drugs that enhanced his strength and fighting skills. He used his new powers to track down and kill refugees from Delvadia in New York. Spider-Man stopped him.

POWER RANK	ENERGY PROJECTION	STRENGTH	DURABILITY	FIGHTING SKILL	INTELLIGENCE	SPEED
	1	3	2	5	2	2

TASKMASTER

Tony Masters—Taskmaster—has worked as a high-priced mercenary and physical trainer for heroes and villains alike. He'll take any job as long as he gets paid. Taskmaster is an expert with every type of weapon, and has mastered all known fighting styles.

Thanks to his ability to copy anyone's moves, Taskmaster is evenly matched against Captain America.

MASTER OF ALL TRADES

Taskmaster is a familiar presence among both the Super Hero and Super Villain communities. Despite his super-powers Spider-Man can be beaten by Taskmaster in one-on-one combat, thanks to Taskmaster's encyclopedic knowledge of the fighting styles of everyone from Captain America to Boomerang.

VITAL STATS

REAL NAME: Anthony "Tony" Masters

OCCUPATION: Sheriff, assassin, mercenary

BASE: Mobile

HEIGHT: 6 ft 2 in (1.88 m)

WEIGHT: 220 lbs (99.79 kg)

EYES: Brown **HAIR:** Brown

ORIGIN: Human born with photographic reflexes; later took an experimental version of the Super-Soldier serum that allows him to instantly memorize motor skills

POWERS: Taskmaster's photographic reflexes mean he can perform any combat move after seeing it once—even Spider-Man's acrobatics! He can mimic voices and use various weapons.

	ENERGY PROJECTION	STRENGTH	DURABILITY	FIGHTING SKILL	INTELLIGENCE	SPEED	POWER RANK
	1	3	2	4	4	2	

...ESA PARKER

Teresa Parker is Peter's long-lost sister, adopted as a baby after their secret agent parents are killed on a mission. As an adult, she is recruited into S.H.I.E.L.D. by Nick Fury Sr., and becomes a top espionage operative. Teresa meets her brother by chance on an operation against the Kingpin, and having discovered her true identity, makes it her mission to catch their parents' killer.

Aided by Nick Fury, Teresa finds proof that she really is the daughter of Mary and Richard Parker, and is Peter Parker's sister.

VITAL STATS
REAL NAME: Teresa Parker
OCCUPATION: Secret agent
BASE: Mobile
HEIGHT: 5 ft 7 in (1.70 m)
WEIGHT: 135 lbs (61 kg)
EYES: Blue
HAIR: Brown
ORIGIN: Human; daughter of Mary and Richard Parker, unknown to her older brother Peter until they meet as adults
POWERS: Teresa is a skilled hand-to-hand fighter and master of numerous weapons; she is also equipped with a flight harness and weapons built by the Tinkerer.

Teresa's guns are equipped with various non-lethal bullets, including ice and taser varieties.

She is also given basic web-shooters for firing web-lines.

TAKING FLIGHT
Peter Parker takes Teresa to the Mason, a secret equipper of heroes who later turns out to be the villain the Tinkerer. Here she turns from spy to Super Hero as she is equipped with a flight suit and customized, non-lethal weapons. This tech augments her already excellent fighting skills, honed through years working for espionage organizations.

POWER RANK	ENERGY PROJECTION	STRENGTH	DURABILITY	FIGHTING SKILL	INTELLIGENCE	SPEED
	1	2	2	4	4	2

THING

Ben Grimm is the Thing, trapped in an unbreakable body of rock ever since the outer-space accident that created the Fantastic Four. The Thing has a big heart and acts as a "big brother" to less experienced heroes. Despite his enormous strength, the Thing isn't shy about teaming up when necessary—he worked with Spider-Man to stop an out-of-control Hulk.

As a close friend of the Fantastic Four, Spider-Man is invited to Ben Grimm's bachelor party.

SOLID AS A ROCK
The Thing is a good-natured presence in the Super Hero community. For years he has run a friendly series of card games where Spider-Man and other heroes can let off steam, get advice from more experienced crime-fighters, and share stories of their adventures.

Before he became the Thing, Ben Grimm was a test pilot and astronaut.

Ben's skin is virtually unbreakable, although it can be pierced by adamantium.

VITAL STATS
REAL NAME: Benjamin Jacob "Ben" Grimm
OCCUPATION: Adventurer
BASE: 4 Yancy Street, New York City
HEIGHT: 6 ft (1.83 m)
WEIGHT: 500 lbs (226.8 kg)
EYES: Blue
HAIR: None (originally brown)
ORIGIN: Human mutate; exposed to cosmic radiation
POWERS: Ben has a rocky hide and massive superhuman strength, stamina, and durability. An exceptional pilot and trained astronaut, he also has great fighting skills.

ENERGY PROJECTION	STRENGTH	DURABILITY	FIGHTING SKILL	INTELLIGENCE	SPEED
1	6	6	5	3	2

POWER RANK

HOR

The God of Thunder and a founding member of the Avengers, Thor is an awe-inspiring figure who sets a heroic ideal for Spider-Man to live up to. Sent to Earth from Asgard by his father Odin, Thor became one of the world's most famous defenders despite the scheming interference of his arch-enemy Loki. His deeds earned him the respect of his father, who later granted Thor the title of All-Father and handed him the throne of Asgard.

The mighty hammer Mjolnir can only be carried by a worthy bearer. Thor can use it to call down lighting from the sky.

VITAL STATS
REAL NAME: Thor Odinson
OCCUPATION: Lord of Asgard
BASE: *Toothnasher*, Newark Harbor, New Jersey
HEIGHT: 6 ft 6 in (1.98 m)
WEIGHT: 640 lbs (290.3 kg)
EYES: Blue
HAIR: Blond
ORIGIN: Asgardian
POWERS: Thor has superhuman powers, great fighting skills, and wields the magical hammer Mjolnir, which enables him to fly, opens dimensional portals, and fires bolts of energy.

Thor wears Asgardian armor.

Thor can harness the energy from storms, even without Mjolnir.

CHAMPION OF ASGARD
Thor has been with the Avengers since the beginning, and encouraged Spider-Man to try out for a spot on the team. He views the web-slinger as a worthy warrior and is happy to fight at his side when the opportunity arises.

POWER RANK

ENERGY PROJECTION	STRENGTH	DURABILITY	FIGHTING SKILL	INTELLIGENCE	SPEED
			5	2	

TINKERER

The Tinkerer is highly sought after within the criminal underworld as a builder of gadgets, weapons, and vehicles. He encountered Spider-Man when creating high-tech gizmos to simulate an alien invasion. The Tinkerer has outfitted many of Spider-Man's foes, including the Beetle, Mysterio, Scorpion, and Trapster.

The Tinkerer's inventions are one-of-a-kind. Their effects are unpredictable, so they can be difficult for Spider-Man to combat.

The Tinkerer sells his inventions to the highest bidder.

His body may be frail, but the Tinkerer's mind is as sharp as ever.

DANGEROUS EVERYWHERE
The Tinkerer has often landed behind bars, but that doesn't slow him down. Within the prison walls he is a king, offering his services to build devices for his fellow inmates and assist them in their escape attempts.

VITAL STATS
REAL NAME: Phineas T. Mason
OCCUPATION: Former criminal outfitter and technician
BASE: Small fix-it shop, New York City
HEIGHT: 5 ft 8 in (1.73 m)
WEIGHT: 170 lbs (77.11 kg)
EYES: Gray
HAIR: White
ORIGIN: Human
POWERS: Tinkerer is a scientific genius who specializes in making deadly innovative weapons from ordinary machine parts.

ENERGY PROJECTION	STRENGTH	DURABILITY	FIGHTING SKILL	INTELLIGENCE	SPEED
1	2	2	2		2

POWER RANK

TOAD

Orphan mutant Mortimer Toynbee developed the extraordinary ability to make tremendous leaps and lash out at foes with his elastic, prehensile tongue. He grew up a tragic loner before joining Magneto's Brotherhood of Evil Mutants for a time—it was Magneto who gave him the name "Toad." Sensing that Toad was not truly evil at heart, Spider-Man befriended him and tried to boost his self-esteem.

Toad's tongue can grasp objects, but this ability isn't enough to win respect from heroes or villains.

VITAL STATS

REAL NAME: Mortimer "Mort" Toynbee
OCCUPATION: Adventurer
BASE: Krakoa, Pacific Ocean
HEIGHT: 5 ft 9 in (1.75 m)
WEIGHT: 169 lbs (76.66 kg)
EYES: Black
HAIR: Brown
ORIGIN: Mutant
POWERS: Toad can make superhuman leaps and is an extremely flexible, agile combatant. He can extend his tongue up to 30 feet (9 meters) in length and use it as a whip in combat situations.

A Jester's costume indicates Toad's sidekick status.

HOPING FOR MORE
Toad formed a Super Hero team, the Misfits, with his fellow outcasts Frog-Man and Steel Spider. Unfortunately, the team didn't impress. Toad continued to look for new ways to apply himself, and eventually fell back in with his old comrades in the Brotherhood of Evil Mutants.

Toad's legs have incredible leaping power.

POWER RANK	ENERGY PROJECTION	STRENGTH	DURABILITY	FIGHTING SKILL	INTELLIGENCE	SPEED
	1	4	3	5	2	3

TOMBSTONE

A towering brute with a vicious streak and teeth filed into sharp points, Lonnie Lincoln carved out a fearsome reputation as mob hitman Tombstone. He had an ongoing vendetta against Robbie Robertson of *The Daily Bugle*, whose evidence saw him jailed for his crimes. After Tombstone escaped from prison, he and Robertson agreed a truce when they discovered that their children were dating.

As an underworld enforcer in New York City, Tombstone hopes to finish Spider-Man once and for all.

VENDETTA
In retaliation for his prison sentence, Tombstone did everything he could to make Robbie's life a nightmare. Spider-Man helped his friend stay out of Tombstone's clutches, though the villain remained a constant threat among the city's criminal elite.

Tombstone is very hard to injure, claiming that his skin is as hard as diamond.

He is a fan of jazz and a regular at legendary Harlem venue Minton's Playhouse.

VITAL STATS
REAL NAME: Lonnie Lincoln
OCCUPATION: Crime lord
BASE: Harlem, New York City
HEIGHT: 6 ft 7 in (2.01 m)
WEIGHT: 460 lbs (208.65 kg)
EYES: Pink
HAIR: White
ORIGIN: Human mutate; was given a chemical concoction to boost his abilities
POWERS: Tombstone has superhuman strength and bulletproof skin. He is an expert with guns and at hand-to-hand fighting.

ENERGY PROJECTION	STRENGTH	DURABILITY	FIGHTING SKILL	INTELLIGENCE	SPEED
1	4	5	4	1	3

POWER RANK

TOXIN

The offspring of Carnage, the alien symbiote called Toxin bonded with police officer Patrick Mulligan as its human host. As it had only recently spawned, the symbiote's nature was not yet fully formed, and Patrick's inherent decency influenced its development. Toxin became a conflicted hero and an occasional ally of Spider-Man. Patrick was later killed by the villain Blackheart so that he could steal the Toxin symbiote.

Along with Anti-Venom, Toxin tries to be one of the few heroic symbiotes.

VITAL STATS

REAL NAME: Patrick Mulligan
OCCUPATION: Vigilante; former police officer
BASE: New York City
HEIGHT: 6 ft 2 in (1.88 m)
WEIGHT: 215 lbs (97.52 kg)
EYES: Green
HAIR: Brown
ORIGIN: Human bonded with symbiote
POWERS: The alien symbiote gives Toxin enhanced strength and healing, the ability to scale walls and shoot webbing, and limited shape-shifting powers.

Toxin heals from injuries quickly.

SYMBIOTE SWAPPING
Control of the Toxin symbiote later passed from Patrick Mulligan to Eddie Brock, who had previously served as the host of Venom. Like Patrick, Eddie tried to control Toxin and use the symbiote's powers for good, hunting down criminals and gang members.

Symbiote forms a second skin over its host.

POWER RANK	ENERGY PROJECTION	STRENGTH	DURABILITY	FIGHTING SKILL	INTELLIGENCE	SPEED
	1	5	5	4	2	3

TRAPSTER

Scientist Peter Petruski, a specialist at inventing sticky substances, was formerly the third-rate crook Paste-Pot Pete. He underwent a Super Villain makeover to become Trapster. A frequent enemy of Spider-Man and the Human Torch, Trapster often works with other criminals as one of the Frightful Four.

If Spider-Man is hit by one of Trapster's blasts, he'll be glued in place.

Goggles protect eyes from adhesive fumes.

GIFT FOR INVENTION
Trapster is one of Spider-Man's most persistent foes. He has a lot in common with the web-slinger, being a chemical genius with a gift for building machines that spray adhesive fluids in the manner of Spider-Man's web-shooters.

Trapster keeps his adhesive in a tank worn on his back.

VITAL STATS
REAL NAME: Peter Petruski
OCCUPATION: Mercenary, criminal; former scientist
BASE: Mobile
HEIGHT: 5 ft 10 in (1.78 m)
WEIGHT: 160 lbs (72.57 kg)
EYES: Brown
HAIR: None (formerly brown)
ORIGIN: Human
POWERS: Trapster is a brilliant chemist whose glues and solvents allow him to walk up walls, immobilize enemies, and fire sticky projectiles that explode on impact.

ENERGY PROJECTION	STRENGTH	DURABILITY	FIGHTING SKILL	INTELLIGENCE	SPEED
1	2	3	2	4	2

POWER RANK

TRAPSTR

The new Trapster, or Trapstr as she later styles herself, is a woman of mystery. Adopting the alias of one of New York City's more eccentric villains, she adds her own twists to bring it right up to date. She does not wear a Super Villain costume, instead favoring a signature look based around a leather jacket, pumps, and tinted goggles that she wears almost constantly.

Trapstr and her Syndicate comrades are among the many villains coerced by Kindred into attacking Spider-Man.

VITAL STATS

REAL NAME: Unknown
OCCUPATION: Criminal
BASE: New York City
HEIGHT: 5 ft 8 in (1.73 m)
WEIGHT: 136 lbs (62 kg)
EYES: Brown
HAIR: Black
ORIGIN: Human
POWERS: Trapstr fires a super-strong adhesive paste from her wrist-mounted guns.

A highly online villain, she is rarely seen without her phone in her hand.

Trapstr carries her paste in back-mounted canisters connected to guns carried on wrist gauntlets.

When Trapstr broke up a fight between Spider-Man (Peter Parker) and Vulture, she dismissed them both as "ridiculous" and "old," to Spidey's horror.

STICKY SCIENCE
Trapstr's paste is not just for sticking her opponents to walls—it is specially formulated to contain reactive particles, enabling her to track anyone she has shot via an app of her own design. In this way she combines old-school science with the cutting-edge developments of the digital age.

POWER RANK	ENERGY PROJECTION	STRENGTH	DURABILITY	FIGHTING SKILL	INTELLIGENCE	SPEED
	1	1	1	3	3	2

TYLER STONE

Tyler Stone is an executive of the Alchemax Corporation in the year 2099, based in the city of Nueva York. As the head of research and development, Stone has access to a world-beating array of technology. An amoral man concerned only with furthering his own wealth and power, Stone made an enemy of his time's Spider-Man (Miguel O'Hara), a scientific genius who is also Stone's illegitimate son.

A time-traveling Tyler Stone finds a way to get at Miguel O'Hara through Miguel's pregnant, paralyzed girlfriend, Tempest.

Ruthless and without sentiment, Tyler Stone personifies the corporate domination of his time.

VITAL STATS
REAL NAME: Tyler Stone
OCCUPATION: Vice-President of Research and Development at Alchemax Corporation
BASE: Nueva York, Earth-928
HEIGHT: 6 ft (1.83 m)
WEIGHT: 185 lbs (84 kg)
EYES: Blue
HAIR: Blond
ORIGIN: Human
POWERS: Although he has no super-powers, Tyler Stone is a master of manipulation.

FAMILY TROUBLES
Tyler Stone's relationships with his two sons, Miguel O'Hara and Kron Stone, are far from affectionate. His own father, Tiberius Stone, was the ruthless founder of the Alchemax Corporation, with links to the shadowy Hand organization as well as the Kingpin (Wilson Fisk).

ENERGY PROJECTION	STRENGTH	DURABILITY	FIGHTING SKILL	INTELLIGENCE	SPEED
1	2	2	1	3	1

POWER RANK

UNCLE BEN PARKER

When Peter Parker's parents Richard and Mary died in a plane crash, Peter's Uncle Ben raised him as his own son. Ben and his wife May loved Peter and taught him the value of responsibility. Tragedy struck when, shortly after Peter gained his powers, he selfishly let a burglar go free—with terrible consequences for Ben.

The guilt he felt over his uncle's death led Peter to pursue a life of great responsibility.

VITAL STATS

REAL NAME: Benjamin Franklin "Ben" Parker
OCCUPATION: Retiree; former textile worker, soldier
BASE: Queens, New York City
HEIGHT: 5 ft 9 in (1.75 m)
WEIGHT: 175 lbs (79.38 kg)
EYES: Blue
HAIR: White
ORIGIN: Human
POWERS: Uncle Ben was a normal human being, but had military training and was an above-average fighter for his age.

The Parkers never had much money, but Uncle Ben didn't let it show.

ETERNAL EXAMPLE
The burglar that Peter had ignored later killed Uncle Ben. Peter vowed that no one would ever suffer such a tragedy again, and committed himself to fighting injustice as Spider-Man! Uncle Ben has continued to serve as Peter's spiritual inspiration from beyond the grave.

POWER RANK	ENERGY PROJECTION	STRENGTH	DURABILITY	FIGHTING SKILL	INTELLIGENCE	SPEED
	1	2	2	1	2	2

VALERIA RICHARDS

The daughter of Reed and Sue Richards, Valeria Richards is a budding genius and one of Spider-Man's friends in the extended family that is the Fantastic Four. Doctor Doom assisted at Valeria's birth and secretly put a spell on her, which later allowed him to control her. Fortunately, Reed managed to break the spell.

Despite growing up in the unusual environment that surrounds the Fantastic Four, Valeria has a down-to-earth and playful personality.

The Thing has taught Valeria the basics of hand-to-hand combat.

UNLIMITED POTENTIAL
Valeria is still developing her super-powers. Like her father Reed Richards, she is showing early signs of genius-level intellect in a variety of fields. Peter Parker, who is a scientific genius himself, believes Valeria could be a scientist with Horizon Labs when she gets older.

Valeria is smart enough to figure out how to use the Forever Gate to go anywhere in space and time.

VITAL STATS
REAL NAME: Valeria Meghan Richards
OCCUPATION: Adventurer, scientist
BASE: 4 Yancy Street, New York City
HEIGHT: 3 ft 4 in (1.02 m)
WEIGHT: 40 lbs (18.14 kg)
EYES: Blue
HAIR: Blond
ORIGIN: Human
POWERS: Valeria has a highly advanced intellect and is considered a genius engineer and roboticist.

ENERGY PROJECTION	STRENGTH	DURABILITY	FIGHTING SKILL	INTELLIGENCE	SPEED
1	2	2	1	6	2

POWER RANK

VENOM EDDIE BROCK

The alien symbiote known as Venom first appeared as a black-and-white version of Spider-Man's costume, with a dark mind of its own. After Spider-Man rejected it, the suit bonded with disgraced reporter Eddie Brock to create Venom, an evil mirror of Spider-Man with shape-shifting abilities. Brock would later also bond with the Anti-Venom and Toxin symbiotes, but was reunited with Venom and tried to become a hero.

His long experience with the alien beings made Eddie Brock an expert in dealing with symbiotes.

VITAL STATS

REAL NAME: Edward Charles Allan "Eddie" Brock
OCCUPATION: God of the Symbiotes, vigilante; former reporter
BASE: New York City
HEIGHT: 6 ft 3 in (1.91 m) (variable as Venom)
WEIGHT: 260 lbs (117.93 kg) (variable as Venom)
EYES: Blue (white as Venom)
HAIR: White; formerly strawberry blond (none as Venom)
ORIGIN: Human turned into the Nexus of the Symbiote Hive-Mind
POWERS: The symbiote has enhanced strength and healing, as well as the ability to shoot webs and scale walls. Venom can control its composition for shape-shifting or camouflage purposes.

Eddie was temporarily given the powers of the God of Light to battle the dark god Knull.

HOST HOPPING
The Venom symbiote has possessed other human hosts besides Eddie Brock. For a time it infected Mac Gargan, better known as the Scorpion. More recently, Venom chose Peter Parker's friend Flash Thompson as its host. As Venom, Flash worked as an official agent of the U.S. military.

POWER RANK	ENERGY PROJECTION	STRENGTH	DURABILITY	FIGHTING SKILL	INTELLIGENCE	SPEED
	1	5	5	2	2	3

As he tries to manage without his father, Dylan is accompanied by two unusual "pets"—Venom in dog form and the Sleeper symbiote in the shape of a cat.

VENOM DYLAN BROCK

Dylan Brock is the son of Eddie Brock, although neither knew it for the first few years of the boy's life. Raised by his abusive grandfather, Dylan reached out to Eddie for help. Discovering the truth about their connection, the two began to build a relationship, and later Eddie gave Dylan his blessing to be the new host of the Venom symbiote.

LIGHT VS. DARK
Dylan is at the heart of Earth's defense against the dark symbiote god Knull. Backed up by the Avengers, Dylan bravely tries to utilize his symbiote powers, but can only overcome Knull with backup from his Enigma-Force-powered father. Eddie then uses his power to purge Dylan of the dark material within him.

Formerly having the power to control symbiotes but not to bond with them, Dylan can now bond with the Venom symbiote.

As the new Venom, he now has all the powers associated with the symbiote.

VITAL STATS
REAL NAME: Dylan Brock
OCCUPATION: Student
BASE: New York City
HEIGHT: 4 ft 8 in (1.42 m)
WEIGHT: 76 lbs (34 kg)
EYES: Blue
HAIR: Blond
ORIGIN: Born to Annie Weying and Eddie Brock using genetic material from the Venom symbiote
POWERS: When bonded with the Venom symbiote, Dylan possesses super-strength, speed, durability, agility, and stamina. He can shapeshift, communicate telepathically with other symbiotes, and has spider-powers.

ENERGY PROJECTION	STRENGTH	DURABILITY	FIGHTING SKILL	INTELLIGENCE	SPEED
1	4	4	2	2	3

POWER RANK

VENOM 2099

The Venom symbiote still exists in 2099, hidden in the city sewers of Nueva York. It finds a host in Kron Stone, son of Alchemax executive Tyler Stone and half-brother to Miguel O'Hara (Spider-Man), and enemy to both. Paired with the bitter and twisted Kron, Venom kills O'Hara's girlfriend Dana before being defeated by Spider-Man using a sonic attack. Fragments of the symbiote are then taken to laboratories at Alchemax.

When Alea Bell becomes the host of the Venom symbiote, she can't resist using her new power to intimidate her school bully.

VITAL STATS

REAL NAME: None
OCCUPATION: None
BASE: Mobile, Earth-928
HEIGHT: Variable
WEIGHT: Variable
EYES: White/red
HAIR: None
ORIGIN: Alien symbiote living in sewers of Nueva York in 2099; later kept in laboratory at Alchemax Corporation
POWERS: The symbiote has superhuman strength, speed, stamina, durability, and agility. It can wall-crawl, shape-shift, and secrete powerful acid.

Unlike the symbiote seen in the past, the 2099 version of Venom has evolved acidic secretions that are powerful enough to burn through Spider-Man's costume.

NEW HOST, NEW START
The Venom symbiote seizes the opportunity when a fragment of it is taken from the Alchemax labs and bonded to an injured teenager, Alea Bell, to heal her. It forces Alea to help it free the rest of its pieces from Alchemax, but when it is whole again Venom agrees to work with Alea to protect others.

When Kron Stone was Venom's host, the symbiote displayed red eyes in a white, mask-like face.

POWER RANK	ENERGY PROJECTION	STRENGTH	DURABILITY	FIGHTING SKILL	INTELLIGENCE	SPEED
	1	4	4	2	2	3

VERMIN

A mad scientist's experiment gave Edward Whelan fur, claws, and a heightened sense of smell. He became the rodent-faced villain Vermin, hiding in New York's sewers and snatching victims for his dinner. Despite his crimes, Vermin desperately wishes to be cured of his rodent curse.

When Vermin acts on animalistic instinct, he views all intruders as enemies and attacks without mercy.

LURKING IN THE DARK

When Kraven the Hunter's daughter Ana lured Spider-Man into the sewer tunnels, Vermin tried to chase the intruders out of his territory. Though Vermin tries to keep a low profile, his ravenous hunger has caused him to prowl the city on the hunt for fresh meat.

Vermin's claws and fangs harbor toxic bacteria.

Only a shred of humanity remains in Vermin.

VITAL STATS

REAL NAME: Edward Whelan
OCCUPATION: Former employee of Ravencroft Institute
BASE: Mobile
HEIGHT: 6 ft (1.83 m)
WEIGHT: 220 lbs (99.79 kg)
EYES: Red
HAIR: Brown
ORIGIN: Human mutate; subjected to genetic experiments by Arnim Zola
POWERS: Vermin's powers are proportional to those of a man-sized rat. He can communicate with rats and summon them to do his will.

ENERGY PROJECTION	STRENGTH	DURABILITY	FIGHTING SKILL	INTELLIGENCE	SPEED
1	4	3	2	1	3

POWER RANK

VINCENT GONZALES

Rookie NYPD officer Vin Gonzales was Peter Parker's roommate and his rival for the affections of forensic detective Carlie Cooper. Acting on orders from high up in the department, Vin planted spider-tracers at various crime scenes to try and frame Spider-Man. After being discovered and brought to justice, he apparently wanted to put the past behind him and move on. However, he was also working for Norman Osborn.

As Peter Parker's roommate, Vin Gonzales quickly found his fate tied up with Spider-Man's. His involvement in a plan to take down the web-swinger backfired badly.

VITAL STATS
REAL NAME: Vincent "Vin" Gonzales
OCCUPATION: Criminal, prisoner; former Police Officer
BASE: New York City
HEIGHT: 5 ft 10 in (1.78 m)
WEIGHT: 182 lbs (82.55 kg)
EYES: Brown
HAIR: Black
ORIGIN: Human
POWERS: As a trained police officer, Vin Gonzales was in good physical shape with expertise in firearms and hand-to-hand combat.

Vin has a Green Goblin tattoo on his forearm.

JUSTICE SERVED
Vin eventually confessed to his role and expressed regret over his part in the conspiracy. As a show of good faith he testified against his fellow plotters within the police force, receiving a reduced prison sentence in exchange for his cooperation.

He is an avid reader of J. Jonah Jameson's anti-Spidey editorials.

POWER RANK	ENERGY PROJECTION	STRENGTH	DURABILITY	FIGHTING SKILL	INTELLIGENCE	SPEED
	1	2	2	2	2	2

VULTURE

Wearing a flying harness he had invented, Adrian Toomes became the costumed criminal the Vulture. The Vulture was one of the first criminals Spider-man ever faced. He is old for a Super Villain, but his hatred of Spider-Man keeps him active. He is a frequent member of the Sinister Six villain team.

The Vulture often enters a building by crashing through a window, using his wings to shield himself from flying glass.

An electromagnetic harness allows the Vulture to fly.

NO REPLACEMENTS NEEDED
Nothing bothers Adrian Toomes more than pretenders who try to claim the Vulture identity for themselves. Despite his advanced age, Toomes is still the best Vulture of them all, and he actively works to sabotage those who would take away his claim to fame.

VITAL STATS
REAL NAME: Adrian Toomes
OCCUPATION: Professional criminal; former electrical engineer, inventor
BASE: New York City
HEIGHT: 5 ft 11 in (1.8 m)
WEIGHT: 175 lbs (79.38 kg)
EYES: Hazel
HAIR: None
ORIGIN: Human
POWERS: Adrian Toomes uses his electromagnetic harness to fly, and he can cut enemies with his sharp feathers. His harness also gives him enhanced strength.

Spider-Man is physically stronger, but can be outmaneuvered by the Vulture.

ENERGY PROJECTION	STRENGTH	DURABILITY	FIGHTING SKILL	INTELLIGENCE	SPEED
1	3	5	2	5	3

POWER RANK

WHIRLWIND

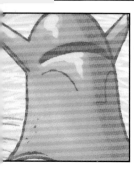

Dave Cannon was a mutant born with super-speed and the ability to spin himself at great velocity. He was also a natural bully, and from an early age used his powers for theft and extortion. Taking a day job as an ice-skater, he began a double life as the costumed criminal the Human Top, later becoming Whirlwind. He occasionally partnered with Trapster, making him one of Spider-Man's many foes.

When fighting Whirlwind, Spidey needs to watch for innocent bystanders who might be injured by flying debris.

VITAL STATS

REAL NAME: David Cannon
OCCUPATION: Professional criminal; former circus performer
BASE: New York City
HEIGHT: 6 ft 1 in (1.85 m)
WEIGHT: 220 lbs (99.79 kg)
EYES: Blue
HAIR: Brown
ORIGIN: Mutant
POWERS: When Whirlwind does one of his trademark spins, he can generate powerful gusts of wind or slash at his enemies with wrist-mounted blades.

Whirlwind can spin at 1,600 revolutions per minute.

REBRANDING
During a confrontation inside *The Daily Bugle* building, Spider-Man gave the former Human Top a new name—Whirlwind—while the two combatants traded insults. Whirlwind liked the name and fashioned a new identity.

POWER RANK	ENERGY PROJECTION	STRENGTH	DURABILITY	FIGHTING SKILL	INTELLIGENCE	SPEED
	4	4	3	3	2	3

WHITE RABBIT

Lorina Dodson is very strange, but she likes it that way! Obsessed with the book *Alice's Adventures in Wonderland*, she began her criminal career as the White Rabbit. Spider-Man knows that the White Rabbit is an unpredictable foe—her past antics have included riding a giant mechanical bunny.

The White Rabbit's crimes make sense in her head, but few others can predict what she'll do next.

Bunny ears are part of the gimmick.

EXPANDING THE WONDERLAND GANG
The White Rabbit is always looking for new recruits who fit her particular theme. During one crime spree she gave a new villain, the Walrus, a chance to impress her and join her gang. Their robberies came to an end when they ran into Spider-Man, Leap-Frog, and Leap-Frog's son Frog-Man.

Lorina is very wealthy, having inherited a lot of money, so she can finance all her bizarre criminal gadgets herself.

VITAL STATS
REAL NAME: Lorina Dodson
OCCUPATION: Professional criminal
BASE: New York City
HEIGHT: 5 ft 7 in (1.7 m)
WEIGHT: 130 lbs (58.97 kg)
EYES: Blue
HAIR: Strawberry blond
ORIGIN: Human
POWERS: While lacking super-powers, the White Rabbit is a creative inventor with talents in engineering, robotics, and explosives. Her weapons are often ridiculous, but no less deadly for that fact.

ENERGY PROJECTION	STRENGTH	DURABILITY	FIGHTING SKILL	INTELLIGENCE	SPEED
1	2	2	3	2	2

POWER RANK

WILL O' THE WISP

Researching the outer limits of the electromagnetic spectrum, Jackson Arvad experienced a life-changing accident that loosened the natural bond between his body's molecules. As Will O' The Wisp, he attacked Spider-Man on the orders of evil mastermind Jonas Harrow.

Will O' The Wisp can travel so quickly he appears as merely a streak of light, making it tough for Spidey to get a bead on him.

VITAL STATS
REAL NAME: Jackson Arvad
OCCUPATION: Former scientist
BASE: Mobile
HEIGHT: 6 ft 1 in (1.85 m)
WEIGHT: 195 lbs (88.45 kg)
EYES: White
HAIR: Blond
ORIGIN: Human mutate; exposed to an intense electro-magnetic field in a laboratory accident
POWERS: Jackson can control his body's composition, giving him the powers of flight, intangibility, and light projection.

FINDING HIS OWN WAY
Jackson later rebelled against his boss, Jonas Harrow, and decided to go into business for himself. Silver Sable recognized the usefulness of Will O' The Wisp's unique combination of powers. She offered him a place on the team of reformed villains called the Outlaws, a position that saw him fight alongside Spider-Man.

The light he emits while controlling his molecules is hypnotic, enabling Will O'The Wisp to control people.

By controlling his density, Will O' The Wisp can become superhumanly strong.

POWER RANK	ENERGY PROJECTION	STRENGTH	DURABILITY	FIGHTING SKILL	INTELLIGENCE	SPEED
	3	4	6	2	3	3

WOLVERINE

James Howlett, aka Wolverine of the X-Men, is a friend that Spidey can count on. Born with a mutant healing factor, Wolverine received the upgrade of a metal skeleton with retractable claws through the top-secret Weapon X program. One of Spider-Man's New Avengers teammates, Wolverine is always the first into battle.

During their time as teammates, Spider-Man and Wolverine gained new appreciation for their different approaches to crime-fighting.

Enhanced senses make Wolverine a master tracker.

EXPERIENCE MEETS ENTHUSIASM
Wolverine's gruff personality might seem at odds with Spider-Man's easy-going attitude, but the two of them make a great team. During Spider-Man's time with the New Avengers, Wolverine became good friends with Aunt May and Mary Jane Watson.

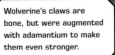

Wolverine's claws are bone, but were augmented with adamantium to make them even stronger.

VITAL STATS
REAL NAME: James Howlett
OCCUPATION: Adventurer
BASE: Krakoa, Pacific Ocean
HEIGHT: 5 ft 3 in (1.6 m)
WEIGHT: 300 lbs (136.08 kg)
EYES: Blue
HAIR: Black
ORIGIN: Mutant augmented with adamantium
POWERS: Wolverine has a mutant healing factor and very sharp senses. His skeleton has been reinforced with unbreakable adamantium and he can extend razor-sharp claws from his fists.

ENERGY PROJECTION	STRENGTH	DURABILITY	FIGHTING SKILL	INTELLIGENCE	SPEED	POWER RANK
1	4	4		2	2	

RAITH

Yuri Watanabe is a respected captain in the NYPD, but she becomes increasingly frustrated by the limitations of official law enforcement and adopts the alias of Wraith to serve swifter justice on the felons who prowl her city precinct. Wraith is an alias intended to terrify criminals, an apparent vengeful ghost who is not bound by the same rules as a police officer.

Wraith wears a mask so that she can pass as dead police officer Jean DeWolff and make people believe she is a supernatural being.

VITAL STATS
REAL NAME: Yuri Watanabe
OCCUPATION: NYPD officer, vigilante
BASE: New York City
HEIGHT: 5 ft 7 in (1.7 m)
WEIGHT: 115 lbs (52 kg)
EYES: Brown
HAIR: Black
ORIGIN: Human
POWERS: Yuri uses various pieces of equipment formerly belonging to Super Villains to confuse and terrify her opponents.

The lenses in her mask have facial recognition technology so she can quickly identify people out in the field.

LOST AND FOUND
Using her access to the police evidence room, Yuri liberates various pieces of Super Villain equipment to help her in her quest. She uses a mask from the Chameleon, various pieces of tech taken from Mysterio, and canisters of Fear Gas formerly belonging to Mister Fear.

Wraith's tendrils have polygraph sensors in them so she can tell if someone is lying.

POWER RANK	ENERGY PROJECTION	STRENGTH	DURABILITY	FIGHTING SKILL	INTELLIGENCE	SPEED
	1	2	2	3	2	2

WRECKING CREW

Thanks to a close encounter with Asgardian magic, four thugs gained the power to level anything in their path—and to make life miserable for heroes like Spider-Man! Forever a team, the members of the Wrecking Crew are always on the lookout for their next big heist.

KEY MEMBERS

1. **Bulldozer:** Superhuman strength, speed, and durability and can crash headfirst through walls.

2. **Wrecker:** Superhumanly strong and swings an indestructible, enchanted crowbar—the source of the Wrecking Crew's power.

3. **Thunderball:** Brilliant scientist as well as having superhuman strength. His weapon is a heavy ball and chain.

4. **Piledriver:** Armed only with his fists but has superhuman strength and is virtually bulletproof.

Wrecker is leader and founder of the Wrecking Crew.

MYSTICAL POWER

The Wrecking Crew have tangled with both Spider-Man and Spider-Woman, but their greatest enemy is the Asgardian God of Thunder, Thor. As their powers are magic-based, the Wrecking Crew's strength depends on the intensity of the mystical energies that flow to Earth from the realm of Asgard.

Senior Editor David Fentiman
Project Art Editor Stefan Georgiou
Senior Production Editor Jennifer Murray
Senior Production Controller Mary Slater
Managing Editor Emma Grange
Design Manager Vicky Short
Publishing Director Mark Searle

Designed for DK by Ray Bryant

This American Edition, 2022
First American Edition, 2014
Published in the United States by DK Publishing
1745 Broadway, 20th Floor, New York, NY 10019

Page design copyright © 2022 Dorling Kindersley Limited
DK, a Division of Penguin Random House LLC
22 23 24 25 26   10 9 8 7 6 5 4 3 2 1
001–332244–Nov/2022

© 2022 MARVEL

A catalog record for this book
is available from the Library of Congress.
ISBN 978-0-7440-6347-9

DK books are available at special discounts when purchased in bulk
for sales promotions, premiums, fund-raising, or educational use.
For details, contact: DK Publishing Special Markets,
1745 Broadway, 20th Floor, New York, NY 10019
SpecialSales@dk.com

This book was made with Forest
Stewardship Council ™ certified paper—
one small step in DK's commitment to a
sustainable future. For more information
go to www.dk.com/our-green-pledge

Printed and bound in China

For the curious

www.dk.com